Connie Potter

DISCIPLESHIP

S0-BDO-000

ACCOUNT ABILITY

Becoming People of Integrity

ACCOUNTABILITY

Becoming People of Integrity

WAYNE SCHMIDT

YVONNE PROWANT

ACCOUNTABILITY: BECOMING PEOPLE OF INTEGRITY
Copyright © 1991 by Wesley Press

Wesley Press
P. O. Box 50434
Indianapolis, Indiana 46250-0434

Library of Congress Cataloging in Publication Data

Schmidt, Wayne and Prowant, Yvonne
    Accountability: Becoming People of Integrity
    Wesley Press: Indianapolis, Ind. © 1991.
    1. Accountability 2. Integrity I.Title
            ISBN: 0-89827-089-8

All Scripture passages, unless otherwise indicated, are from the New International Version © 1987 by New York International Bible Society.

All rights reserved. No part of this publication may be reproduced, stored in a retrieval system, or transmitted in any form or by any means — electronic, mechanical, photocopy, recording, or any other — except for brief quotations in printed reviews without the prior permission of the publisher.

Printed in the United States of America

❑ ❑ ❑ ❑ ❑ ❑ ❑ Table of Contents

Accountability:
Our Experiences

❏ *Wayne's Turn*

I can remember being a little nervous. I was having lunch that day with Paul Anthes, a businessman in our congregation whom I knew casually and deeply respected. Paul is a man of his word and follows through on his commitments.

We were meeting to discuss whether we might become accountability partners, forming a relationship to help ensure that our aspirations made it into actions. I was nervous because I knew the partnership would bring me face-to-face with some issues of personal and spiritual growth.

I rationalized that I was a busy pastor of a large and growing church, so it was understandable that I sometimes neglected my family, missed my devotional times, or worked too many hours. With the pressure I was under, it was excusable to eat too much, sleep too little, or neglect some relationships.

But in my heart I knew these faults were unacceptable and even harmful to being God's man. And I knew Paul was the type of person who wouldn't let me compromise my most important values for the sake of "success." I was nervous because I was stepping up to a new level of accountability and growth.

That luncheon took place late in 1984 and the results have literally changed my life. Nothing, and I mean nothing, has done more for my spiritual and personal growth than accountability. Little by little, God is using accountability in my life to make me more like His Son, Jesus Christ.

As I practiced accountability in my life, it became a conviction I began to share with others. I challenged our congregation in person and group meetings as well as from the pulpit. Others have caught the vision and put accountability into practice in their lives.

This book has been written with the desire to more adequately equip people to implement personal accountability. It is designed as a "how-to" book. My prayer is that through its pages we might stimulate others to increase their accountability and grow in becoming more like Christ by putting God's Word into action.

❏ *Yvonne's Turn*

I had been attending Kentwood Community Church for only a short time when I heard Pastor Wayne Schmidt first preach about accountability partnerships. I listened somewhat skeptically. My husband and I had both already developed a deep respect for Pastor Wayne personally and for his preaching. But this concept was one I had to think about.

Perhaps it would work for people who weren't very self-motivated or who didn't have goals. But I didn't think it was for me. I had always had goals. I always strived to be the best. I really didn't need someone to "check up on me." I didn't honestly think it would motivate me further to have someone to whom I would actually have to answer; or so I thought.

Shortly thereafter, all my brothers and sisters gathered in Ann Arbor to keep a vigil at the hospital where our Dad's life hung in the balance following a major heart attack. My sister, Kathy, and I are close, though different in some ways. One way in which we are different is in our attention to detail. She is a computer programmer and very detail-oriented. I am a manager; I like to deal with the "big picture."

To pass the time, I decided to balance my checkbook — something I did only every two or three months. I always knew "about" how much money I had. As Kathy watched me juggling all those statements and old registers, she was appalled and did not hesitate to tell me about it. I think her lecture said something about how someone who supervises a busy emergency

department, organizes programs, and holds positions of leadership in organizations should be more responsible in her personal finances. She couldn't believe I knew only "about" how much money we had. She challenged me to get it in order and informed me that when we came for Thanksgiving she would be asking me for my checkbook to see if the balance was current. Fine.

I really didn't think much more about it until we were within fifteen minutes of her home on our Thanksgiving trip. Suddenly I remembered that she was going to ask for my checkbook and it had not been balanced since I had last seen her. So I hurriedly began adding and subtracting. My husband, Mick, questioned me as to why

I was balancing the checkbook all of a sudden — something he rarely saw me do. I replied that Kathy would be asking to see it.

This was one of those experiences that occurs to me when I hear a concept or theory and then sometime later something happens that causes that concept to come to life. So this was what Pastor Wayne was talking about regarding accountability partners — being motivated by knowing that someone who matters would be checking to see that I had done what I said I'd do. It's true that if Kathy would not have been checking, I don't know when I would have balanced my account again!

I began to think about other areas of my life. Sure, I was quite productive. But were there other areas in which I didn't do what was required? Well, there was my weight — it was just such a struggle. And what about the evaluations that were often late because I put them aside to do something more creative or interesting? But I was responsible for getting them in by a certain date and the employee's raise was delayed if I didn't. Would it make a difference if someone would help me keep a check on the due dates and how many reports were outstanding? Just maybe. I began to realize that maybe there was more to this concept than I had originally thought. Sure, I'm self-motivated, but not for the areas of my life that don't come naturally or that don't interest me much.

So I got involved in an accountability partnership and found that, sure enough, it did help to have someone encourage me in the areas where I needed encouragement and to challenge me in some other areas.

Sometime later, Mick and I were members of a leadership development team. One task of this team was to pick a goal for the life of the church and develop an action plan to accomplish that goal. We identified the area of accountability and stated a goal that fifteen percent of the Kentwood Community Church constituents would be involved in an accountability

partnership. We identified the supports and barriers. From this experience, one of our steps was to develop a class to teach people the "how-to's" of developing an accountability partnership. We worked with Pastor Wayne to find out more about the accountability aspect of it and combined that with sound management principles of determining values, priorities, and goal setting. After all, if these concepts worked for corporations, why wouldn't they work for individuals?

Pastor Wayne had already formed a group in the church called the "Accountability Roundtable." The purpose of this Roundtable was for partnership members to meet to share ideas, to ask questions of other partnerships and, in general, to gain support from one another for continuing in the accountability partnership. It proved to be very valuable for the members that had participated.

There were a number of people in our church who had heard much about accountability, but didn't know how to take the next step. Therefore, the accountability class was developed to take people through the process to teach them the principles but, most importantly, to give them an opportunity to practice how to be accountable to another person. The class incorporated both the accountability principles and principles of determining values, goals, and action plans. The class time proved to be very valuable in this regard. For those of you who will be taking the class in addition to reading this textbook, I encourage you to put the principles into practice one by one as you learn them.

It was as a result of this class and the feedback from the class participants that the idea for this book was born. It is our hope that many will begin accountability partnerships which will in turn strengthen their walk with the Lord. As one of the class participants said "I know I'll answer to the Lord someday, but in the meantime it would help if I had somebody in the flesh to keep me in check." That is the whole idea of an accountability partnership: someone with whom you agree to meet for the purpose of reviewing your goals, asking questions, and helping you to become the person you want to be based on your stated values and priorities.

This book is designed to look at the biblical basis for accountability. After looking at the biblical basis for accountability, we will take a look at how to determine our values, goals and priorities and then develop an action plan. These tools are useful to keep you on track when you meet with your accountability partner. Establishing an accountability partnership, looking for a partner, sharing information with each other, recognizing when the partnership should be ended and putting the partnership to rest are

additional topics covered. Each chapter in this book as well as the activities of the accompanying workbook builds on the previous one. Greatest benefit will be gained if concepts are followed in order.

Introduction

It was a small article in our local paper, tucked in one of the inner sections. The headline and content were nothing that drew attention. Most people probably didn't even read it. However, one line in the article caught my eye. I will never forget it. "Our past history with Mr. _____ is he doesn't do what he says he's going to do." Quite a reputation!

This article dealt with Mr. _____ 's request to the planning commission for a zoning change. Their decision affected the future of his business. It went on to describe the previous behaviors that led to a public conclusion that he wasn't a man of his word. Even his lawyer was quoted as saying that "his client didn't have the greatest track record."

Most of us don't have a public reputation of not keeping our word, but what about our private lives? How are we at doing what's important rather than what's urgent? How are we at being accountable in the areas that aren't visible for public scrutiny?

Yvonne Prowant

2

Accountability:
An Overview
Yvonne Prowant

"Many of us can go on about our business everyday without really being watched or without anybody asking us to answer for our behavior. When we agree to become accountable we agree to give an answer to, or give a reason for our actions. This might include asking and answering some hard questions, both of ourselves and of our accountability partner. It is in effect a willingness to be watched."

Think back for a minute to the goals you had when you were younger. How many of those goals have you achieved? Did you even have specific goals? Think back to five years ago. Now think back to last New Year's Day. New Year's Day is a time when we typically make new goals for the coming year that are called resolutions. What resolutions did you make? How far into the new year did you continue to actively work on them? How many of your resolutions have you accomplished? Which of them has been on your list for several years in a row, but without much progress? Now let's look at last week. What did you tell yourself or tell others that you would do for them or with them? Did you do it? Your answers to these probing questions will probably be a combination of "yes" for some of the goals and "no" for others.

Most of us probably have a fairly long list of good intentions that never became realities. Think for a minute about the goals that you did achieve. What kept you working toward that goal? What about the goals that never became reality? What kept you from reaching those goals? As I review the goals that I have set and never met, I can identify one of two reasons why those goals never became reality. Either the goal didn't turn out to be all that important to me after all, or I ran into obstacles along the way, became discouraged, and quit. There is a cycle or a pattern that happens when we set goals and run into obstacles. I'll call this a "Commitment Failure Cycle." We have much energy, put forth effort, but then run into obstacles. When we first run into obstacles, we make a new commitment and put forth more effort. But if we continue to run into obstacles, we will eventually become discouraged and give up. Look at the illustration below:

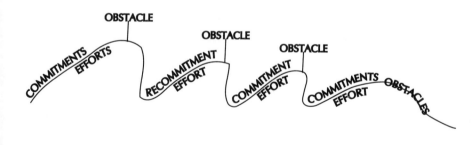

The initial commitment is made with a lot of energy and the next commitment after the obstacles is met with less energy. As you meet more and more obstacles, there is less and less energy given to the new commitment until you finally reach a status-quo or a "stand still" state where

there are neither commitments nor obstacles. This state is more comfortable than having to deal with failure over and over.

When we repeatedly meet obstacles and then let go of goals, we get "wiser." To avoid the pain of failing, we simply stop making commitments. Have you ever noticed how people in different stages of life make commitments with differing degrees of energy and enthusiasm? When I was twenty, I made commitments with the idea that I could conquer the world. In our twenties, my friends and I were not apathetic when people asked us if we wanted to be committed to something; we responded with energy and determination. And then I noticed as I approached thirty that I became wiser; I became more reserved in my commitment. I began to do a little more evaluating before I said a ready "yes." I had been impacted by ten more years of reality. I had run into some obstacles and met some failure. My offers had not always paid off in the achievement of my goal. As I look now at friends and family who are in their forties, fifties, sixties, and even seventies, I see people who make fewer and fewer commitments in an effort to avoid the sense of failure. Most of us avoid personal pain, including emotional, if given a choice. We look back now at the eager, younger generation with a smug "you'll learn" attitude.

❏ *Breaking This Process*

Rather than "wise up" and stop making commitments, it would be great if there was a way to deal with these obstacles as they occurred and continue working toward our goals until we achieve them. When we set a goal or make a commitment, people should be able to count on us to follow through. What if our characters were so mature that our actions were consistent, regardless of the circumstances? The key to having this happen can be found in accountability.

In this process of commitment, obstacles, and failure, an accountability partner is valuable. He/she is there when you meet the obstacles to help solve problems, give encouragement along the way, or just stand by and be a friend as you continue toward your goal without giving up. An accountability partner would be your encourager or advisor along the way toward the achievement of your goals.

❏ *What is Accountability?*

We hear much about accountability now, as a result of some people who have failed due to a lack of accountability. The recent United States savings and loan institutions crisis can be traced to a few people in responsible positions who were not accountable for their actions. As a result of their decisions and behaviors, many people suffered and even the national economy was affected. Integrity is crucial.

Accountability means to be responsible for, to answer for, or to give an explanation for our actions. Most of us do not have to give an explanation for our actions. Many of us can go on about our business everyday without really being watched or without anybody asking us to answer for our behavior. When we agree to become accountable, we agree to give an answer to, or give a reason for our actions. This might include asking and answering some hard questions, both of ourselves and of our accountability partner. It is in effect a willingness to be watched.

Recently a Los Angeles driver was arrested and an area resident videotaped the arrest, without the knowledge of the arresting officers. The officers were videotaped as they assaulted and beat the driver of the automobile. The person who had made the videotape turned it in to police authorities and it became public knowledge. These officers are now being held accountable because someone was watching them. They cannot justify their actions, they cannot excuse what they did, and they cannot alter the facts. This is a vivid example of being held accountable for inappropriate behaviors and actions even when we don't realize anyone is watching. Our goal in accountability partnerships is to have someone be "willing to watch us" for the purpose of keeping us on track.

❏ *Examples of Accountability*

Don't be scared away at this point. Accountability is something that most of us aren't used to doing. Or are we? There are many examples of accountability relationships, some which we choose and some which are imposed on us. Think about the following situations:

1. Highway driving. We're all bound by the same laws of the road. Consider speed limits. What percentage of the time do you stay within that

limit? What do you do when you see a radar gun or a patrol car in your rear view mirror? If you're anything like me, one of your immediate, almost reflexive, reactions is to step on your brakes and then check your speedometer — in that order.

Think of how your driving would change if someone were always watching you. Then how often would you obey the speed limit?

2. Employee/employer relationships. Each of us is responsible for a certain task, regardless of our position. If no one ever checks on us or gives us feedback on how we're doing, what happens? Do you ever get the idea that no one really cares about how you perform? Do you ever slack off because you "worked so hard last week" or because the boss is out of the office? As a manager of a hospital emergency department, I sometimes put on my scrubs and work in the clinical area as the charge nurse. I like that. It keeps me in touch with the clinical skills, the patients and the staff whom I supervise. Whether I'm there or not, things run quite smoothly. However, I'm told that there are a few people who perform differently on the nights when I'm there than they do on the nights when I'm not there. Does that surprise me? Not at all. I think it takes a tremendously motivated person to do what is expected whether or not he or she thinks anyone will know.

3. Weight loss clinic. To help me reach my goal for physical fitness, I joined Weight Watchers. This organization recognizes the value of feedback regarding reaching goals. Before I joined, I could envision my weight being announced in front of the whole group and then hearing condemnation or praise, depending on my progress. Actually, it is much different. The weigh-in is private, but very effective. It is confirmation of how I know I've done during the week. Those scales don't lie! Anyone is invited to share his or her loss or gain, and the group is supportive. I pay to be accountable to this group for weight loss. I've tried several ways to lose weight without this accountability. Those ways just didn't work for me.

❏ *Biblical Example*

One of the most graphic biblical illustrations of accountability can be found in the life of Joseph. When he was faced with temptation by Potiphar's wife, he responded by saying:

17

"With me in charge, my master does not concern himself with anything in the house; everything he owns he has entrusted to my care. No one is greater in this house than I am. My master has withheld nothing from me except you, because you are his wife. How then could I do such a wicked thing and sin against God?" (Genesis 39:8-9 NIV)

He was accountable to both Potiphar and God, though he had the opportunity to have even more — and who would have known? He knew to whom he was accountable and to whom he would have to answer!

❏ *Types of Accountability*

1. Mentor accountability. One person is involved in teaching another. In educational settings, we are accountable for attaining certain skills before we are promoted. The Wesleyan Church has a program in which an experienced pastor is paired with a less experienced pastor for the purpose of mentoring. They meet regularly for this process.

2. Spouse-to-spouse accountability. Standards are established in each relationship for what each spouse is responsible for and what would be acceptable or unacceptable in each relationship. Part of that might come from either discussion or official agreements before the marriage. Spouse-to-spouse accountability is different from the accountability partnerships which we are talking about here. In one of the later chapters we will explain why spouses are not the best accountability partners for each other.

3. Third party accountability. Two persons agree to meet with a third person for the purpose of review and feedback.

4. Group accountability. One is accountable to a group for a particular purpose. Examples of this include college study groups, Bible study groups, and Bible study fellowship groups. If you have participated in one of these groups, you know what it's like to go to the meeting without having completed your assignment. I was always greatly motivated to be prepared because of the expectations of group members.

5. Spiritual leader accountability. "Obey your spiritual leaders and submit to their authority. They keep watch over you as men who must give an account" (Hebrews 13:17).

6. Ultimate accountability. There is no choice. Ultimately we are all held accountable to God Himself. "So then, each of us will give an account of himself to God" (Romans 14:12).

One-to-one accountability. Two people, by mutual agreement, form a partnership for the purpose of holding each other accountable for that which they choose to share with one another.

This book will deal primarily with the "one-to-one accountability partnership." Principles that are explained apply to the other types of accountability as well. Topics include: "How to develop a one-to-one accountability partnership," "Questions participants ask" and "Testimonies from those having benefitted from being an accountability partner."

❏ *What Makes An Accountability Partnership Work?*

Many factors have been identified that will help an accountability partnership be more effective. One is that when a goal is shared with another person, the probability of its achievement increases. Prior to working in an emergency room, I thought that anyone who attempted suicide would automatically be hospitalized. This is not true. One evening I asked one of the mental health workers what the criteria was for hospitalizing a suicidal patient as opposed to discharging him or her. How could you predict who would go home and be okay and who would go and complete the act of suicide? He explained that one crucial factor is whether the suicidal patient will make a pact with another person that he/she will not attempt suicide again until a certain specified time, which is usually after an appropriate therapy can be initiated. They know that when a goal is made with another person or shared with another person, it greatly increases the probability that the goal will be reached.

Another factor is that a partner is a person who can be an encourager as we start toward the accomplishment of a goal. Most of us will meet obstacles. When we do, our accountability partner will be there to help encourage us, help us solve problems, and help us keep a healthy perspective of the obstacles. Obstacles then become hurdles to cross rather than barricades that stop us.

A third factor is that an accountability partner helps you stay "focused" on your goals. When you meet with someone every week or two to review progress toward your goals, there isn't much time to lose track of where you're headed. You can then make wiser choices about what you do and how you spend your time so that you are focused on the activities that you

consider to be priorities.

In Ephesians 5:21 we read: "Submit to one another out of reverence for Christ." The word submission has taken on some negative connotations in recent years but, in fact, it is a liberating term. When you voluntarily submit, you are in control. No one makes you submit; it is something you choose to do. In the case of the accountability partnership it is a covenant with a fellow believer to provide discipline in reaching specific personalized objectives. This concept is really the essence of the accountability partnership because you are the one who decides what your values, priorities and goals are, and you then ask someone to keep you on target.

My accountability partner is what the name indicates — a partner. She serves to reinforce the goals I have set. If I learn from her or we become close friends, these are added blessings. I am primarily relating to her, though, for the purpose of discipline — in order to reinforce my will power.

❏ *Accountability: What's In It For Me?*

Why would anyone want to be accountable? Life is getting more difficult daily. Why not take the easy way out? Won't accountability just add something else to an already hectic schedule? There are numerous benefits in having an accountability partnership. It's important to look at the benefits and costs together so that you can make an informed choice about whether or not this partnership is something in which you would like to get involved. This kind of partnership is not for everyone. But for those who do choose it, the following benefits will result from your commitment:

1. It prevents excesses which might result from isolation. In other words, when we live in our own little world and no one is allowed into our world or we are not required to give an answer for any of our actions, we could develop excesses in certain areas of our life which would not be healthy or beneficial.

2. It strengthens our personal integrity. Commitment helps me avoid procrastination. When I meet with my partner every two weeks and I say that I am going to do something by a certain date, I'm held accountable to reach that deadline. And if not, I need to give an answer for that, or at least,

in my own mind, come up with a reasonable explanation.

3. It helps develop discipline.

4. It enhances your role as a model for Christianity, both to family and others.

5. A more fruitful life is evident.

6. Problem solving will help prevent little problems from becoming major issues.

7. It provides encouragement when the going gets tough.

The benefits of accountability are not limited to the two people involved in the partnership. It extends to family, friends, co-workers, neighborhoods and anyone with whom we have contact.

❏ *Results Of Accountability*

The benefits of having an accountability partnership go beyond personal growth. There are results that will impact our family, social and work relationships, and even our neighborhoods. They are:

1. Growing personally
2. Building up the body of Christ
3. Furthering God's kingdom on earth

❏ *Growing Personally*

There are many factors that contribute to our individual growth — circumstances, trials, challenges, personal relationships, life events. When someone is there to help us look at the situations, to encourage us, or to help us solve problems, we have a greater chance of growing as a result of the situation. After a certain age, physical growth stops but emotional and spiritual growth doesn't. Even though it doesn't stop, it is not automatic growth.

21

❏ *Building Up The Body of Christ*

There are also benefits to the Body of Christ. The results of people having accountability partnerships is that as we each grow individually and become stronger in our Christian faith, this is evidenced as people observe the church as a whole. You've no doubt heard it said that a chain is only as strong as its weakest link. While I hesitate to refer to the Body of Christ as a chain, it is true that each of us has an individual responsibility to the Body of Christ. This is best illustrated for us in 1 Corinthians 12:12, 14, 24b-27:

"The body is a unit, though it is made up of many parts; and though all its parts are many, they form one body. So it is with Christ . . . Now the body is not made up of one part but of many . . . But God has combined the members of the body and has given greater honor to the parts that lacked it, so that there should be no division in the body, but that its parts should have equal concern for each other. If one part suffers, every part suffers with it; If one part is honored, every part rejoices with it. Now you are the body of Christ, and each one of you is part of it."

Each of us has a part and is accountable for doing that for which God has designed us. Perhaps you don't know what it is that God wants you to do. Maybe you've heard about spiritual gifts, but don't know what yours are. In our chapter on spiritual life accountability we will help you to identify the areas in your spiritual life for which you should be accountable. If you do know what God wants you to do, how are you doing? Would it help if you could share that information with someone else and talk with him/her about it on a regular basis?

As the body of Christ becomes stronger and as each of us becomes more accountable for the things God would want us to do, the kingdom of God is advanced. We are called to be the salt of the earth and the light of the world. As we are living by the Holy Spirit, the fruit of the spirit is evidenced in our lives: love, joy, peace, patience, kindness, goodness, faithfulness, gentleness and self-control (Galatians 5:22). As this fruit becomes evident, it will impact those around us. Romans 14:17-18 puts it this way:

"For the kingdom of God is not a matter of eating and drinking, but of righteousness, peace and joy in the Holy Spirit, because anyone who serves Christ in this way is pleasing to God and approved by men" (NIV).

What a contrast to the life of the hypocrite! Hypocrisy is pretending to

have feelings or characteristics that you really don't possess; in other words, you are just playing a part or acting. The kingdom of God can be hindered by those who "play the part" of Christianity. The onlookers are almost never deceived. Hypocrisy opens the church to one of the greatest criticisms of Christians today and is used as an excuse by some for not taking a serious look at the gospel. How would your life be different if you were willing for someone of your choosing to talk with you about your spiritual walk? What if they had the freedom to share an area where they saw that your walk did not match your talk? An accountability partner would be that person — with your permission.

❏ *Count The Cost!*

The benefits of an accountability partnership outweigh the costs, but like anything that's worthwhile, the costs must be considered:

1. Time. In order for an accountability partnership to be effective, there must be a mutual time commitment. The amount of time is as individual as the partnership. Most of the partnerships of which I'm aware meet from one to two hours every one or two weeks.

2. Pride. Meeting with someone and being honest with that person requires a certain amount of humility. He/she is going to be the one to help us in the areas where we struggle. The partnership won't be effective if we don't honestly share with him/her. "As water reflects a face, so a man's heart reflects the man." (Proverbs 27:19).

3. Comfort zone. There is a certain comfort that surrounds us as we settle into the daily tasks in our circle of family, friends, and work relationships. As we begin to stretch and grow in some areas of our life, we might not be as comfortable as if we just relaxed in the "status quo." Even though the "status quo" may not be our ideal, it's so comfortable!

The discipline of accountability at times may seem unpleasant, but the life it produces is most fulfilling. The benefit of an accountability partnership is that you grow while having the privilege of contributing to the growth of another.

❏ *Steps To Accountability*

If you weigh the balance between costs and benefits and decide to

proceed, there are several steps that can lead to an effective accountability partnership:

1. Personal relationship with Jesus Christ
2. Desire to please Christ and a willingness to grow
3. Decision to grow and make wise choices
4. Personal assessment
5. Establishment of values, priorities, goals
6. Choosing a partner
7. Meeting regularly with your partner
8. Annual audit

Each of these will be explained in great detail later on so that you will be able to build an effective accountability partnership. In the next chapter, Pastor Wayne shares the biblical perspective.

❏ *For Your Consideration:*

At the beginning of the chapter several questions were asked. A few ideas probably came to your mind as you were reading. Now, really think about past promises, goals or good intentions. List five goals or "good intentions" you've had in the past.

Place a Y (Yes) or N (No) beside each of them to indicate whether or not they became a reality.

Review your list you just made. For those that did not become a reality, what obstacles got in the way?

❏ ❏ ❏ ❏ ❏ ❏ ❏ ❏

For those that became a reality, what encouragement or factor contributed to their accomplishment?

List two examples of situations in which you are held accountable (i.e. obeying laws, paying taxes).

What is the consequence if you are not accountable?

Name two people who would benefit from being held accountable.

It is often easy to think of others who need to be more accountable. What areas of your life would benefit from having an accountability partner to encourage you and check on your progress?

What part of your personality or character could lead to failure of left unchecked?

□ □ □ □ □ □ □ □

What would keep you from having an accountability partner?

Are you willing to explore this concept as a method for personal growth?

3

"Two Are Better Than One!"

Accountability: A Biblical Basis

Wayne Schmidt

"Accountability helps prevent the urgent things in life from displacing the important things . . . an accountability relationship prods us to reflect on life as a whole, a perspective from which we can better determine what is most important."

Talk about a guy who has it all . . . probably one of the most successful men who ever lived. His personal wealth would certainly qualify him for the Forbes list of the world's richest people. He counts among his investments precious metals, shipping freighters, plantations, and extensive personal residences. Many speculate his holdings are so vast that he is not even aware of all that belongs to him. He doesn't spend it all on himself, but contributes to public works programs, religious institutions, and other charitable causes.

Added to his wealth are the people he knows. He is personally known and respected by the leaders of the worlds' governments. He socializes with the "beautiful people." He is invited to all the parties that are attended by the wealthiest and most influential people.

But it doesn't even stop there — added to his financial and relational accomplishments is his intellectual prowess. He has studied and reflected upon all dimensions of life. There are people who come from all over the world to seek out his wise perspective on life. Some would certainly say he

was the wisest man who ever lived!

Now this is a self-sufficient person — not in need of anyone or anything. If there was ever a person who could live independently of others, it must be he. We could speculate that he must certainly be an advocate of the rugged individualism that we treasure so dearly and trumpet so loudly in our Western culture. We're shocked, then, when we hear him quoted:

"Two are better than one, because they have a good return for their work: If one falls down, his friend can help him up. But pity the man who falls and has no one to help him up! Also, if two lie down together, they will keep warm. But how can one keep warm alone? Though one may be overpowered, two can defend themselves. A cord of three strands is not quickly broken." Ecclesiastes 4:9-12 (NIV).

What is Solomon saying? In a word, get the most out of life when we share it with another person. We share our lives through relationships at home, at church, in our neighborhood, and at our workplace.

"Two are better than one" — that is the real basis of any accountability relationship. Christ demonstrated it when He sent His disciples out two by two. The early church sent its missionaries in teams — Paul and Silas, Paul and Barnabas, Barnabas and Mark, to name but a few. We can live life most effectively and fully when we unite and work with others.

In fact, this passage gives us four reasons that "two are better than one."

❏ *Two Can Be More Productive*

"Two are better than one, because they have a good return for their work"
(Ecclesiastes 4:9, NIV).

One of the disciplines which I hold as a deep conviction is the reasonable maintenance of my physical condition. I try to monitor my diet, engage in regular exercise, and get a proper amount of sleep. It's important to me, but I've never been accused of being a fanatic!

While I've been regularly exercising for years, it is still not on my list of best-loved activities. My natural inclination is toward dormancy. I envy those animals who get to hibernate all winter! What has been the key to maintaining this discipline? I regularly work out with others. On the days I don't feel like it, I know they'll be waiting for me. When I'm tempted to pedal slowly, they push me to pick up the speed. When I want to skip the scales, they look over my shoulder to check my weight. I'm convinced that in spite of the fact that fitness is a deeply held conviction, without their

nudging (or nagging), I'd be overweight and out of shape. They offer me accountability.

Accountability prompts us to get the tough things done. It is tough when what we value goes against our grain. Consider:

❏ having devotional times when we are tired
❏ dating our spouse when the schedule seems too busy
❏ completing an assignment when we'd rather procrastinate
❏ confronting a person or situation we would rather avoid

Accountability reinforces our will power so that we make the tough choices and do the tough things.

It's not, however, just a thumb in our back — it's a pat on the back. Victories are sweeter when they're shared with someone who cares for us. Knowing you'll have someone to celebrate with can urge you on to accomplish what otherwise might be left undone. Those moments of celebration give us the confidence and courage to continue to meet our goals.

Accountability helps prevent the urgent things in life from displacing the important things. Left to ourselves, the pressure of immediate demands may cause us to move back-burner issues to the front-burner, even if they are not worthy of immediate attention. An accountability relationship prods us to reflect on life as a whole, a perspective from which we can better determine what is most important.

Many of the most productive aspects of our personal growth are not highly visible to others. They are, however, the qualities that refine our character — issues like honesty, humility, and holy desires. When these struggles are shared with an accountability partner, and then victories are celebrated together, it helps create positive peer pressure. Sometimes we adults think we leave behind the influence of peer pressure at the conclusion of our teen years. Not so! Even the most self-sufficient adults still feel the impact of peer pressure.

In addition to my personal accountability partnership, I meet for accountability with a small group of men. All are people of influence in their various careers, and all are pressured by the business world to compromise their convictions. It is refreshing for them (and me) to meet with each other for mutual encouragement and reinforcement in a world continually chipping away at spiritual and moral values. It is a setting in which ethics and integrity in the workplace are respected. We have created a setting of positive peer pressure important to all of us.

For Christians, being productive is more than a pleasant option to

consider. It is a command! We are expected to bear fruit as evidence of our connection to the True Vine (John 15). Accountability assists us in fulfilling this God-given imperative.

❏ *Two Can Overcome Failure*

Two are better than one, because . . .
"If one falls down, his friend can help him up.
But pity the man who falls and has no one to help him up!"
(Ecclesiastes 4:9-10).

Wouldn't it be great if spiritual life and personal growth were a matter of one victory after another? That's an idealistic view of life and the Christian's walk. The truth is that between the mountain peaks are valleys, scattered among the high times are low times, and our list of aspirations includes those unreached as well as reached.

We know that God stands ready to forgive our sins and minister to us in our failures. We even know that God uses our failures to develop our character, to keep us humble, and to increase our awareness of the need to depend on Him. Our failures may actually prepare us to be more successful in the future.

We also need encouragement from other people during times of setback and failure. We need a friend who can come alongside us and help us see the light at the end of the long dark tunnel.

Jackie Robinson was the first black man to play major league baseball. In the early days of his illustrious major league career, Jackie faced hostile crowds in every ball park. One day while playing at his home park in Brooklyn, he made an error. The Dodger fans began to boo Jackie mercilessly. Jackie just stood there, devastated, while the fans kept on yelling insults at him. Then shortstop Pee Wee Reese ran over and put his arm around Jackie. The fans quickly stopped shouting, and, as he later confided, Jackie's career was saved.

We at times require an arm around the shoulder, a friend by our side, a personal Pee Wee Reese. An accountability partner can be that person.

Tragically, even the Christian community sometimes has the ugly and ungodly habit of kicking a person when he/she is down. As many have said, soldiers in the Lord's army are the only ones who shoot their wounded.

Sometimes Christians quietly delight in the suffering and shortcomings of another, revealing that the "fruit of the Spirit" in their lives has gone rotten and been replaced by envy, jealousy, and competition.

Failure must never become final! Failures can pave the way to success. An accountability partnership can encourage us to pick ourselves up, dust ourselves off, seek forgiveness if we've sinned, get our focus back on the Lord, and look to the future. We need not be known for our failures. Nor are we failures as people because we've failed in performance. Consider the example of Abraham Lincoln:

Event	*Age*
Failed in business	22
Ran for Legislature-defeated	23
Again failed in business	24
Elected to Legislature	25
Had a nervous breakdown	27
Defeated for Speaker	29
Defeated for Elector	31
Defeated for Congress	34
Elected to Congress	37
Defeated for Congress	39
Defeated for Senate	46
Defeated for Vice President	47
Defeated for Senate	49
Elected President of the United States	51

We remember him today not for his list of failures, but for the person he became as he overcame failure.

When we face failure alone, we tend to regularly engage in pity parties. We may feel defeated and want to quit trying. We may even demean and reject ourselves — forgetting that our value in God's eyes is not based on performance. Accountability keeps us from moping in our despair and groping in darkness — it gets us hoping for what the future can bring by the grace of God!

❏ *Two Can Avoid Isolation*

Two are better than one because . . .
"If two lie down together, they will keep warm.
But how can one keep warm alone?"
(Ecclesiastes 4:9, 11).

The point of this verse is a little more difficult to understand, and I see it speaking to a deeper issue than others might. On the surface, the writer seems to say that if you put two bodies together, they keep warm. This is a truth teens seem to grasp early in life!

But we live in the age of warm waterbeds, electric blankets, and other modern technological warming devices. We no longer need another person to keep warm. What is the meaning for us today?

There is a warmth that goes beyond the physical experience, and that is a relational warmth. It is the warm-hearted feeling that comes when people share their lives openly and honestly with one another. We've all felt the difference between being given the "cold shoulder" and a warm welcome. There are marriages that are cold and amount to little more than peaceful co-existence, while other marriages are intimate, deep, and heart-warming. Some parent-child relationships resemble a cease-fire agreement in a war zone, while other parents have a mutually nurturing and fulfilling relationship with their children. There are churches that leave us cold, while other churches exude an atmosphere of love, acceptance, and forgiveness.

There are lots of lonely people — not only in the world, but in the church; sometimes even in our own homes. Men are often conditioned by society or family to be private and performance-oriented, to the point that sharing feelings and love is perceived as weakness. Women are also experiencing greater pressure as career pursuits often contribute to increased isolation.

Loneliness can have a devastating effect on a person's life. It is no mistake that throughout history, one of the most stringent forms of punishment has been solitary confinement. It breaks a person down, often causing him or her to come unraveled. We will probably never experience solitary confinement in a prison, but for some, the feeling of loneliness is just as great. Loneliness can leave us emotionally and spiritually vulnerable, creating a void or vacuum we may seek to fill in various ways:

❏ young adults frequent singles bars to socialize with others
❏ a spouse, feeling lonely and uncared for, becomes entangled in an adulterous relationship
❏ a teen, seeking approval from others, experiments with drugs or

alcohol
❏ a middle-aged adult spends large amounts of money on counselors, not because he is seeking to grow, but because he is seeking a caring relationship
❏ a pastor, feeling neglected by others, forms inappropriate attachments in a counseling relationship
❏ a businessman compromises his ethical standards to keep a client or an account
❏ a person, believing no one cares, ends his or her life

A warm relationship of integrity and accountability is insulation from the cold winds of adversity and temptation.

Accountability relationships don't always begin with deep sharing of feelings. That's fine. Initially it is appropriate to be cautious about what we share. An atmosphere of trust must precede vulnerability. And trust is earned as a person demonstrates his or her trustworthiness over a period of time. As trust gains momentum, the empty feelings of isolation evaporate. The long-term benefit of accountability is the blessing of a warm and open relationship.

❏ *Two Can Find Protection*

Two are better than one —
"Though one may be overpowered, two can defend themselves.
A cord of three strands is not quickly broken" (Ecclesiastes 4:12) .

There is greater security and protection through unity. This is true in battle where fighting side-by-side or back-to-back (to cover blind spots) gives a greater chance for victory. It's also true that a rope made of interwoven strands is less vulnerable to being broken.

We who know Christ are engaged in a spiritual battle — one that we can fight boldly because of the resources He provides. He has made available to us spiritual armor (Ephesians 6:10-18) and He who is in us is greater than the enemy who opposes us (1 John 4:1-4).

Part of Christ's provision for our protection is our uniting together with other believers. Accountability is the "safety net" for persons who sometimes do not know their own hearts. It is a relationship that helps us to identify the blind spots that we fail to see in ourselves. We can easily develop weaknesses, excuse quirks in our personality, or neglect areas of spiritual growth we will likely overlook without the help of another.

We can become afraid to let people know our struggles. We are tempted to erect a facade because we believe others may think less of us. What if they should discover we still are wrestling with issues we feel should be behind us at a certain point of spiritual maturity! We may think "If they knew 'this' about me, they wouldn't love or respect me."

It is easy to rationalize our attitudes or behaviors. Christians can get caught up in knowing God's Word, not for the purpose of obedience, but in order to be more capable of rationalizing their disobedience in pious-sounding terms. In an accountability relationship, we can accept gentle confrontation, break the cycle of rationalization, and get on with the joyous business of pleasing God.

As the old saying goes "You can't see the forest for the trees." Often we get so caught up in the daily grind that we fail to see life from the long-range, eternal perspective. We downplay the consequences of today's actions and their impact on our lives not only immediately, but eternally.

There is wisdom in many counselors. Important decisions should be brought not only before the Lord, but before people who know the Lord — and us — well. In accountability relationships, there is protection from doing things that are destructive to our walk, or just plain stupid. Accountability may prevent sins of commission (doing something we should not) as well as sins of omission (not doing something we should).

One of my desires is to serve the local church where I am pastor for a long time — maybe a lifetime. The vision God has given me and my congregation will take many years to become reality. Some years back I sought out the advice of a friend who happened to be a district superintendent in The Wesleyan Church. I asked him for keys to effective long-term pastorates. The first one he mentioned was the importance of personal growth — professionally and spiritually. As he put it, "a growing church needs a growing pastor." But I'll never forget his second piece of advice — "don't do anything stupid." He went on to explain how many pastors, in a vulnerable moment, do something stupid that compromises their credibility and often causes them to forfeit their ministry.

Accountability helps me with both areas. It keeps me growing and stretching as a person. And it helps prevent my acting impulsively or blindly. It reinforces my spiritual willpower in battling temptation and keeps negative emotions from permeating my private world and resulting in negative actions.

❏ *Forging A Partnership*

> Two are better than one — because they
> can forge a partnership that brings
> ❏ productivity and effectiveness to life
> ❏ recovery from failures and setbacks
> ❏ intimacy and concern that wards off loneliness
> ❏ security and protection from both sin and stupidity

An accountability partnership benefits not only the individuals involved, but their families, churches, businesses, and communities.

One of the movements that most positively transformed society took place in England two centuries ago. At the center of this movement was John Wesley — known for many strengths, not the least of which was his personal discipline. The early movement called Methodism highly valued relationships of accountability. Wesley was an organizational genius, and although very flexible in his designs, he was singular in purpose:

But in one essential aim, counseling and confirmation through reciprocal oversight, he remained unmoved. It was his firm adherence to this essential principle, and by this concentration upon that which was really important he showed his natural capacity for leadership.[1]

"Counseling and confirmation through reciprocal oversight" is good, old-fashioned terminology for accountability.

Wesley's organization within the Methodist movement was arranged in the following groups — the Society, the Class, and the Band. The bands were small cells of either men or women gathered for pastoral care. Usually consisting of six people, each band was asked four questions at every meeting:

What known sins have you committed since our last meeting?

What temptations have you met with?

How were you delivered?

What have you thought, said or done, of which you doubt whether it be sin or not? [2]

These are not the typical questions you're likely to overhear in the lobby of a church! We end up talking about everything but the issues most crucial to our spiritual lives.

While the questions may need to be changed, the principle is constant: We need accountability relationships in order to experience change in our

lives and to change our world.

Take a look at your life! Have you ever longed for a relationship that really makes a difference? Have you craved a partnership that helps you through the tough times and make the most of the good times?

It's the time for action — getting priorities in focus, goals set, and relationships built that will make your dreams of pleasing God and feeling good about yourself a reality. Two are better than one!

❏ *For Your Consideration:*

When Christ first sent out the disciples, he sent them out by twos. The same is true of the early missionary journeys. What reasons can you think of for this practice? What advantages might there be for twosomes?

People often complain that the "urgent" crowds out the "important." How might being accountable for important commitments help prevent this common problem? Can you think of somehting important you've been wanting to do but its just not getting done? Would accountability help?

Accountability can help prevent personal failure from becoming lasting defeat. Restoration is an important ministry for the Christian. What do the following verses have to say about restoring someone who has fallen?

Galatians 6:1-2

Matthew 18:15-17

❑ ❑ ❑ ❑ ❑ ❑ ❑ ❑

Accountability relationships can help prevent loneliness — the feeling that you're facing life's challenges in isolation from others. How might feeling alone effect a person:

❑ in times of temptation?

❑ in times of discouragement?

❑ in times of celebration?

What are ways in which people rationalize sinful or harmful behavior? Can you think of times of rationalization in your own life? How does accountability combat rationalization?

Wesley's "bands" began their meetings with four questions listed on page 35 of this chapter. How do you think most people would respond to this kind of questioning in today's church? Scripture says we are to confess our faults to one another and pray for one another. How might we fulfill the command today? How might accountability be part of the answer?

---

[1] Martin Schmidt, *John Wesley: A Theological Biography*, Volume II, Part 1 (Nashville: Abingdon Press, 1972), pp. 99-100.

[2] Howard Snyder, *The Radical Wesley* (Downers Grove: Inter-Varsity Press, 1980), p. 36.

4

Values, Personal Assessment, Priorities

Yvonne Prowant

"SUCCESS lies in doing not what others consider to be GREAT, but what you consider to be RIGHT." — John Gray

"There is a way for us to channel our energies toward those areas that we consider to be most important; the things we really value. When we have a clear idea of our values and priorities, the choices about daily activities become easier."

The above quote is inscribed on a plaque that hangs in my office and which was given to me when I graduated from college. I think often about what it means and sometimes I am prompted to examine my motives and my actions as to whether they are great or right or both. Bill Gothard teaches that success is "not determined by what we are but rather by what we are compared to what we could be. It is not measured by what we have done but rather by what we have done compared to what we could have done."

Success means different things to different people. Some people assume that we have achieved success when a certain position in our career or social group has been attained or a certain social status has been achieved. Many times social status and material possessions are used as a measure of one's success. But what is success? Is it related to happiness? Are

successful people necessarily happy? Are happy people necessarily successful? I have come to the conclusion that success means doing what I consider to be the priorities of my life and when I get to the end of a road, looking back and not regretting the choices that I've made.

This idea of success is very closely tied to accountability. Why? Because it is your accountability partner that will help you achieve the areas you consider to be priorities. He/she can even help you sort out all the activities and demands on your time and help you focus your energy so your priorities are where you spend your time.

❏ *Priorities*

The place to start is to figure out what you consider to be the most important interests of your life. Then take a look at yourself, which is what we call personal assessment. When we do a personal assessment, we take a look at where we currently are as compared to where we want to be. Such assessment will help you determine your daily activities so that they are in line with what you think is most important. As of right now, how many of your daily activities are related to the areas of your life that you would consider to be most important?

In *Tyranny of the Urgent* by Charles E. Hummel, we are reminded that most of our activities are what would be classified as urgent rather than important. In contrast, those activities that we consider to be most important often get put off, or never done, because those urgent tasks continue to scream for our attention. Boy, does that sound familiar. Many of my day-to-day tasks could be described as urgent rather than important. Take, for example, the laundry. The laundry is something that needs to be done every day at our house. If more than two days go by without the laundry being done, a large laundry pile and empty drawers result. In the "big picture" of my life, I would classify the laundry as unimportant, yet it consumes a fair amount of my time on a weekly basis. If it is not done, it screams for my attention. It is an urgent task.

On the other hand, I would rate quiet times with my children individually as very important. However, many a day goes by when the urgent tasks have screamed for my attention and my time was directed toward them — the laundry, cooking, or running errands. The important tasks, such as taking time for my children or having my personal devotions, have been put off until a later time. In doing this I run the risk of putting them off day after day until at some point in time they have no place in my

life at all or I look back and think "Boy, I should have really done this" or "I really wish I had done that." At that point, as I was saying earlier, is when I might look back and have regrets.

There is a way for us to channel our energies toward those areas that we consider to be most important; the things we really value. It is by first of all determining our values and priorities and then setting goals and ordering our daily schedules to reflect them. When we have a clear idea of our values and priorities, the choices about daily activities will become easier. "No" may soon become a regular part of our vocabulary. When requests for our time do not fit in with our priorities, the answer should be "no." We are the only ones who can make this judgment call.

My conviction about this idea of choices being based on priorities was put to a test recently. I was nominated to run for the Board of Elders at our church. I thoroughly enjoy the kind of activities an elder position requires: committee meetings, decisions that can be tough, and strategic planning and problem solving. It would be somewhat of an honor, for no woman has been elected before — perhaps this would be the year. I knew what some of the issues that faced our church were and some of the plans that had been made. We were even going to be starting a new building project. So what was the problem? Why didn't I just accept? Because I sensed a conflict in my priorities. I prayed about it and asked others for their counsel. When it comes to big decisions like this, I don't want people to flatter me or just agree with me. My accountability partner focused on the issue. She said "I think you're capable and in fact, I'd like to see you on the board. But I challenge you to decide where you will take the time from that will be required for this commitment." I knew that was the issue. Time! As I looked at my priorities and my current time commitments, I knew from where it would have to come — my family. Yes, I could do it all, but it would be at the expense of a prioritiy that I consider to be number two, right behind my relationship with God.

As hard as it was to decline the nomination, I knew it was the "right" choice. There will be other opportunities to serve on the board. The needs of my family at this particular stage and ages right now will not happen again. I know I will not look back and regret not being on the board. However I might look back and regret the consequences of not meeting the needs of my family. I can't take that risk.

In this chapter you will identify values, set priorities and assess your personal situation. You will use this personal assessment in the next few chapters as you set specific goals.

❑ *Values*

Values are those beliefs, standards or precepts which we consider to be most important. In other words, statements that reflect how you feel about a particular area of your life. One of my value statements has to do with my family. It says: "I value close family relationships and regular times alone together." I also value close ties with extended family members including aunts, uncles, cousins and grandparents. Another one of my value statements has to do with my spiritual life — "I value a Christian commitment that is reflected in my daily activities and is a seven day a week, twenty-four-hour, way of life rather than something we do at church or on certain days of the week." Christianity, for me, needs to be a personal relationship with Jesus Christ that my children can learn from and my friends and family can observe. These are just two examples of what I consider to be values.

Organizations all have values and some even write them down and advertise them to the consumer. A grocery store near our home really values its customers. They have slightly higher prices, but many people shop there anyway. When asked why, they often cite the service and friendly staff. What kinds of things do they do because they value the customer? Here are some examples: The baggers always carry the groceries to the car. Staff members are friendly and helpful. When the baggers go to our cars, they provide umbrellas in rainy weather and snow scrapers in the winter. For regular customers, no ID is needed to cash checks even for several dollars over the amount of the purchase. They provide coffee and public restrooms. These are all ways they show they really value the customer.

St. Mary's Health Services, where I am employed, has long had the reputation of being the hospital where something was different from the rest. But few could express this difference in words. When they tried, "caring" or "compassion" were the words frequently used. Recently a task force was appointed to identify five core values which make the hospital what it is. The group identified: compassion, integrity, quality, stewardship, and innovation. Our value of compassion is modeled by the service to many of the underprivileged in our city. Our motto of "Where caring for is caring about" reflects this compassion and care that we value. Values make a difference in how the business is carried out and values in our personal lives make a difference in how we act.

What about your church? Churches have values also. There's probably nothing built more on values than our churches. But how many of them actually identify or state their values and then base their ministry on those values? Values identification was one of the features that appealed to me

about Kentwood Community Church when we first started attending. They had identified three values and communicated them to all those who attended — ADORATION of the Father in worship, ACCEPTANCE of others in the process of being created anew by God, and ACCOUNTABILITY for growth in this process. You see, when values are clearly identified, decision-making becomes easier. In the case of the church, everything from forms of worship to types of programs available is based on these values.

Values are not limited to corporations or other organizations. Each of us has values that govern our individual lives as well. Values affect all areas of our life — education, finance, material possessions, personal relationships, social memberships, and community activities. How much do you value status? family? church? friends? Think about these questions both in relationship to yourself and those whom you know. Can you guess what some of the values are of others? What kind of factors went into your guessing other people's values? Many of us base those assumptions on how people act, where they spend their time, where they spend their money and the things that they say.

Recently my dad died. Prior to officiating at the memorial service, his pastor gathered with family members to learn more about my dad. He had known my dad for only five years since moving to their community and he wanted to know more about the man before he became sick. We sat around Mom and Dad's living room where we had all been raised and began to tell him who my dad was. I was amazed at how easy it was for us to say what our dad valued. He valued primarily three things. He had a love for God, he loved his family, and he had an incredibly intense work ethic. He also passed those values on to us children. Then we began to give him examples, one right after the other of how Dad demonstrated those values in his life and how he taught us as children. We stopped talking about Dad and looked at each other. What if this were one of us today that people were trying to remember? What would they say? We began to share with one another how we perceived the other person's values. That experience turned out to be a very valuable time for us as a family to talk about the kind of values that we have, what we had gotten from Mom and Dad and what we were going to pass on to our children.

Certain items have relative value depending on the circumstances. One evening Chuck McCallum from Indiana Wesleyan University was a guest speaker at our church. For the purpose of illustration he asked our pastor to come to the platform. He then described a scene and asked Pastor Wayne to imagine that he was fifty stories above a busy street in New York City with a beam between two buildings. Would Wayne cross this beam for one thousand dollars? He quickly declined! The offer was increased to one

hundred thousand dollars. Pastor Wayne, not so quickly this time, again declined. Then the situation changed. What if Jan (his wife) and Jordan and Christoffer (his sons) were on the other side? Without a moment's hesitation, Pastor Wayne agreed to go across. What does he value? The value of a significant amount of money seemed quite insignificant as compared to the value of his family.

❏ *State Your Values*

Write down some of the things that you value most. State them in ways that assume they are already happening. Here are some areas to consider: spiritual, educational/mental, family, vocational, physical/health, financial, social, attitudes, integrity, discipline, time management, civil responsibilities and recreation. You will notice in the study guide that there is a personal assessment tool that deals with each of these value statements.

For each category, write down what you value in that area. Most of us aren't used to thinking in terms of specific value statements, so it may not come easy at first. Don't worry about grammar or format; just write down what you think is important in each of these major areas of your life.

❏ *Personal Assessment*

A personal assessment is a chance for you to take a look at where you currently are. It is an attempt to take stock of your personal situation by taking an inward look in the areas of life we have just listed and determining where you are in each of these areas. Again this is not something we are used to doing but it is extremely valuable for us in the growth process and in determining our goals so that our accountability partner can encourage us in those areas. This is a private exercise and will only be useful if you are totally honest with yourself. It should not be pessimistic or optimistic, but simply realistic. It might be interesting though, if you're brave enough, to ask someone who knows you well and whom you trust to give you some feedback on how they see you in some of these areas.

It is from this personal assessment that you will develop goals in response to the next chapter. Take a few minutes now to go over the assessment tool. It sometimes works best if you just read the question and jot down your first response. In doing this personal assessment, you'll be

able to see areas of strength, needed growth areas and the areas that are holding their own.

❏ *Priorities*

When my husband and I were in college, I remember that even though we had almost no money, we still managed to buy most types of sports equipment that were available. We valued physical activity and we enjoyed sports. Having sports equipment was a priority. A friend of ours was the youth/music director at our church. We were all in the same financial state — broke! It was interesting to note that even though she owned no sports equipment she had almost every kind of musical instrument, recording, and gadget that she could get. Though we both had limited funds, we found a way to get the items that were a priority for us. As I look around, I realize that is true for most of us. It has been several years since we were in that financial state. Thankfully, it has improved. But our possessions still reflect in some ways our priorities. This year Mick and I drive two cars — one is thirteen years old and the other is eight years old. While driving a new car is not a priority for us, we own three computers. What is a higher priority for us? You see, most of us can afford whatever we consider to be the highest priority.

Priorities are intensely personal. There is a home in the countryside that is in obvious need of repair. Last summer, a new pool was constructed in the back yard and stood in stark contrast to the run-down house structure. It seemed to me that the owner had his priorities mixed up. Why would he spend money on a new pool when the house needed repair so badly ? I asked him, but not so bluntly. I discovered his reasoning. He has five children and works long hours. This pool would allow his children to swim all day long even though he would not be home to take them to the lake or to the town pool. He considered this to be most important since there was little else to do in the country. The point? We are in no position to make judgments about others' priorities; they are based on their values.

How do you spend your time? That is another reflection of your priorities. Now, more than ever, it is predicted that time will emerge as our most precious resource — more so than money, food, oil or anything else. Time is limited — yet we are each given the same amount. Man, in all his wisdom and technology, has not been able to figure out a way to increase his time.

The Bible speaks much about time and how it is to be used. God also

speaks about the consequences of poor time management. Our time reflects what we consider to be priorities. It is important to us to use our time wisely. "Be careful how you walk, not as unwise men, but as wise, making the most of your time . . . ." (Ephesians 5:15-16 NIV).

There was a period a while back when I was feeling frustrated. I decided to analyze my activities and try to figure out the source of my frustration. I drew two bar graphs as illustrated below. I listed all the areas of my life in which I felt successful and gave them an appropriate length on the bar to illustrate the degree of success that I felt. On the other graph I drew bars that illustrated what I considered to be my priorities. You see that they are almost exact opposites. Those areas of my life that I considered successful were not the areas of my life that I said I considered to be priorities.

I pondered this for quite a while. I still couldn't figure out the source of my frustration. I asked my husband, Mick, to take a look at it. He quickly pointed out that I had omitted the biggest source of my frustration and he encouraged me to do a similar bar graph that showed where I spent my time and energy. Sure enough, this time graph matched my success graph! My time, more than my words, told the picture of what my real priorities were. I needed to make some adjustments.

❏ *Determine Your Priorities*

When you do a personal assessment, you are setting the stage for your future growth. In determining your priorities, take a look at your personal assessment and identify the areas of strength as well as needed growth areas. Then pick out the ones you consider to be most important. When I do this I have two criteria for making something a priority. First, any area on my personal assessment that I have determined is a priority or high value (and yet I have scored myself low in it) makes it something I need to work on right away. The other criterion that I have for making an area of my personal assessment a priority for goals is that I am currently doing okay on it, but if I don't continue working on it, it will become a problem area. That's how I determine what I would consider to be a priority. Take a look at your list and you'll have to make your own decisions about what your priorities are. What I would like you to do right now is to take a look at your value statements and your personal assessment and jot down three to five priority areas of your life. Please include both positive and negative ones. We shouldn't just be identifying those things where we need work. Most of us would become very discouraged if we only looked at the areas where we

46

needed work. So please identify three to five areas of your life that you would consider priorities. It is this information that we will use in the next chapter when we determine goals.

Once you know what your values and priorities are, you are ready to write some specific goals that you want to achieve. It might seem like we have taken a detour from the accountability partnership, but these are the initial steps. It is hard to have someone hold you accountable if you are not sure of your real priorities or what is important to you. Therefore, we help you establish your values, priorities and goals and then develop an action plan to accomplish this. By doing this, you allow your accountability partner to help you accomplish what you set out to do.

❏ *For Your Consideration*

What are some of the ways in which you measure whether or not someone is successful?

How do you decide if you have achieved success?

What needs to happen before you will consider yourself successful?

❏ ❏ ❏ ❏ ❏ ❏ ❏ ❏

List five urgent and five important tasks that you do.

Urgent	Important
1.	1.
2.	2.
3.	3.
4.	4.
5.	5.

What are your values related to:
  a) spiritual matters?

  b) education?

  c) physical health?

  d) family relationships?

  e) financial?

  f) social?

  g) educational?

If someone were to examine how you spent your time, what would they assume were your top two priorities?

If someone were to observe how you spent your money, what would they assume were your top two priorities?

5

GOALS

Yvonne Prowant

Most people don't plan to fail . . . they simply fail to plan!

"More than anything else, goals help us focus our energies and resources for a common purpose. Without a goal, time and energy is often wasted."

Relax. Go out with a friend. Take a walk. Work out. Watch TV. Take the day off.

All of these options could be written on the faces of a pair of dice that I could keep on my dresser. It would be silly to wake up each morning, roll the dice and, based on chance, do the activities that land on top. Even though this sounds silly, how many of us wake up and have little more direction for our day than the usual activities that demand our time or do whatever comes our way? We all need a few days per year which are somewhat unstructured, but most days we should be taking control of our time so that we do the activities which we consider to be most important. One way to take control is to establish goals.

Goals are statements of where you want to be at a certain time. In working through this accountability process, these goals should flow from your value statements and priorities. Write a statement that describes where

you want to be for a certain area of your life at a particular time. For example, "By three months from now I will have lost ten pounds." or "By six months from now, I will have begun spending at least one evening per week with my family."

The following are criteria by which every goal should be measured. Goals should be: achievable, action-oriented, time-defined, specific, measurable and personal. Here's what I mean.

ACHIEVABLE: Is it possible to accomplish this goal in the time stated? If your goal is to become an astronaut, do you have the capacity to learn the skills? If you are retired and want to fulfill your buried dream of becoming a doctor, is that realistic? I once heard a preacher proclaim in November that he was going to lose forty pounds by Christmas. While I agreed that it was necessary, I didn't think it was realistic!

ACTION-ORIENTED: What will you do about your goal? What verbs describe the action you will take? These verbs help move it from a wish to a goal. Try to finish this sentence — "I will . . ."

TIME-DEFINED: When will this action be so common that it is a regular part of your behavior? At what point do you want to re-evaluate yourself in this area?

SPECIFIC: What exactly will you do? What specifically do you want to accomplish? General goals are hard to achieve because they do not describe a specific target.

MEASURABLE: How will you know whether or not you've accomplished your goal? There should be a clear way to measure your progress. In many cases, get it so specific that you can decide whether you reached your goal or not by answering "yes" or "no."

PERSONAL: These goal statements should all begin with the pronoun "I." You cannot set a goal that requires a behavioral change by another person. Saying that your spouse will pay more attention to you or that your daughter will keep her room clean is out of your control. If your goal involves another, focus on what you will do in the situation.

❏ *"Correctly Stated" Goals*

Here are a few examples of correctly stated goals:

1. By three months from now I will have personal devotions five times per week.

2. By six months from now I will reserve one night a week for family time.

3. By six months from now I will have lost eighteen pounds.

Look at each of the above goal statements. Are they specific, time-defined, action-oriented, achievable, measurable, and personal? In each statement, the answer to all the "qualifiers" is yes.

❏ *"Incorrectly Stated" Goals*

Now look at the following goal statement that are stated incorrectly.

1. I want to grow in the grace and knowledge of Jesus Christ.

2. Our family needs to be closer and spend more time together.

3. I've just got to lose some of this weight.

Ask the same questions. Specific? time-defined? action-oriented? achievable? measurable? personal? None of them qualify in each area.

❏ *Focus*

More than anything else, goals help us focus our energies and resources for a common purpose. Without a goal, energy is wasted without achieving the desired results. Perhaps you remember the 1950's comedy series "The Three Stooges." In one episode the boys were going to build a house. They had no particular plan in mind. Each one arrived with a variety of lumber, supplies, and tools. When they were done, about the only thing that could be said was that it was a structure. Soon the walls came tumbling down and the show ended. If they would have had a plan and focused their energies toward a common goal, the walls would have stood strong. It wouldn't have cost anymore or taken longer (even with planning time), but the end result would have been better.

My dad was a farmer. Early in childhood each of us children helped out with the work of the farm and "got promoted" to the more difficult tasks as age and ability permitted. I'll never forget one lesson Dad taught me when I learned how to chop stubble. This was a process where we used a tractor with a mower behind it. The field was cut into sections and then mowed, much like a yard but on a much larger scale. I was always puzzled as to how a farmer could head into the middle of the field and go in a straight line

to the other side. There were no markings that could be seen or any boundaries. How did it end up so straight?

I can remember this lesson as if it had happened yesterday. I was sitting in the big tractor seat with my feet stretching to reach the pedals. Dad was standing to my left so that he could show me what to do and then ride a few rounds with me to be sure I would be okay. As he put his strong arm around my shoulder, he leaned close to my face and pointed to a tree on the other side of the field. "See that tree?" he asked. "It's almost directly across from us. Keep your eye on that tree and start driving toward it. Don't look down to see what the chopper is doing or don't look back to see if what you've done is straight. Just keep your eye on that tree. When you get there, then you can look back. If you do that you'll always drive in a straight line." I shifted to drive and accelerated. I was tempted to look down but I remembered what he had said. I kept my eyes glued to the tree. Sure enough, when I reached the other side and looked back, my row was as straight as an arrow flies! "Remember this," he said, "It will always work."

Dad wanted to get me started on some of the bigger tasks of the farm, not teach me profound philosophy or spiritual truths. Yet he taught me more than he realized. A few years later, I was reading the Bible. I came across Luke 9:62 (NIV) where "Jesus replied, 'No one who puts his hand to the plow and looks back is fit for service in the kingdom of God.'" The minute I read it I knew exactly what was meant. I had learned that lesson many years before. Jesus was talking about keeping our eyes on Him. Dad had taught me to keep my eyes focused on where I needed to be.

When I was in college, I needed to keep my eye on my goal of becoming a nurse. It reminded me of why I was willing to do without a few "extras", have a very limited budget, spend most of my free time studying and function with limited sleep. I had to have a good reason for borrowing more money than I was making. If I would have stopped midway and focused on my immediate situation rather than my goal, common sense would have told me to quit. Keeping my eye on becoming a nurse kept me on target and willing to endure some temporary discomforts.

Consider travel. We usually start by determining a destination. Then we consider what time we need to be there. Think about starting out in a car with no particular destination in mind. You could waste a lot of time and gas and still not end up at the right place. Like travel, knowing the destination (what the goal is) leaves you options (train, plane, car) as how best to accomplish it. In the next chapter, I'll share how to list all those options and decide on one action plan.

❏ *Mutual Goals*

When we decide on our goals, it's important for us to be aware of the principles of synergism and antagonism. In physics these two principles deal with the action of forces working together. In goal setting, these same principles can be the crucial factors in either achieving our goal or ending up frustrated.

Synergism refers to two actions that, when they occur at the same time, work together to achieve a single result. For example, when you bend your arm at the elbow, the biceps muscle group in the front portion of your upper arm shortens while the triceps muscle group in the back of your upper arm lengthens. Bend your arm a few times and feel these actions. These muscle groups work together to make your arm bend at the elbow. Antagonism means that two actions work against one another. If both of these muscle groups were to shorten or lengthen at the same time, bending your arm would be impossible. The actions would be in competition with one another. The same principle is true for goals. When two or more goals work against each other, progress is hampered.

For our personal goals, it is important that we are aware of nothing that is actually working against the goals which we are trying to accomplish. For example, one of my personal goals is to spend one night per week with my family. I need to be sure that my goal in this case is compatible with each of my family member's goals as well. If they do not desire that night alone or if their schedules do not allow for it, it will be a frustration to me to try to always arrange this time every week where the family is sitting down and having a good time. If I have a goal to achieve an academic or business position which will require additional evening and weekend time, I need to be sure that my husband and family will support me in this goal or at least that it is not in conflict with (particularly) my husband's personal goals. In summary we need to be sure that our goals will work with others' goals that they might impact, not work against, them.

❏ *A Church's Illustration*

Consider a church where the goals of the ministry were not shared by everyone who had the power to make decisions. There seemed to be two groups. One group shared a common goal of ministering to a community of

people from differing ethnic backgrounds who lived in the immediate vicinity of the church. This community of people, in general, was of a lower socio-economic class than the regular constituency of the church. The other group wanted to move the church to the suburbs and start a new ministry focusing on people in those new areas of growth who would naturally be closer to the constituency both in distance and type of people. These two goals were working against each other. There was not a shared common goal.

Pretend now that you're in a board meeting and are called upon to help make some decisions for this church. For instance, shall we hire an associate pastor from an ethnic background similar to those in the immediate vicinity and provide housing for him/her on this street? The answer to that question depends on which "group" you belong to and your goal. One person replies, "If we're going to move to the suburbs in five months and sell this building, why don't we just wait and let the new congregation develop a ministry to these folks? In fact, that's a great idea! Let's look for a congregation of a similar ethnic group to buy our current building."

Another person counters "Well, I think God put us here to minister to the people around us. You're all familiar with the Bible verse that says "Do you not say, 'Four months more and then the harvest' I tell you, open your eyes and look at the fields! They are ripe for harvest" (John 4:35). That's what we should do! You can come here any evening and see all kinds of kids outdoors all over this neighborhood. Let's hire a person with whom they can identify and who can minister to their needs. If we wait to sell the building and let another congregation begin to minister, it might be another year. That might be too late for some of these." How is this issue going to be resolved? One of two ways: either each group comes to an agreement on a common goal or the life and harmony of the church will suffer. Think of the challenge to the pastor who's trying to lead this church! It's like a tug of war. Two goals that oppose each other will never contribute to progress.

❏ *Goal Analysis*

In writing out goals it is important to take the process two steps beyond the actual statement of what you intend to do. The first is to identify why the goal is important to you. The second is something that in management theories is called "force field analysis." That is, what forces are driving the

situation in one direction or another? An illustration to describe this process is that of an airplane in flight. There are different forces being exerted on every area of the aircraft — gravity is pulling it down, thrust is moving it forward, and air resistance is impeding its forward motion. The net result of all of those forces is that the plane is either moving forward, decelerating or descending, standing still, or crashing.

There are also "forces" that affect each area of our lives. We will analyze our goals by identifying the supports contributing to the achievement of the goal and the barriers which keep the goal out of reach.

The first step in stating why this goal is important helps you see if it is worth the effort required to achieve it. It will also serves as a motivator or reinforcement when the going gets tough. The second step of identifying supports and barriers helps you see why you are where you are. These supports and barriers will be the basis for deciding on an action plan.

❏ *It Works*

On New Year's Day, my husband and I sat down with our ten-year-old and six-year-old to set one family goal for the coming year and work through the process until we had a plan of action. Everyone agreed that our goal would be to keep the house neat and clean. The kids were active participants right from the beginning of the discussion. In responding to the question "Why is this important?", some suggestions included that we would be able to find our things when we looked for them, that we could invite friends over without worrying about what the house looked like, and that if we kept things picked up, we'd have more time to do the other things we liked. Well, at least we all agreed. The goal was important enough to do something about it!

We proceeded to the next step. What are the things that help keep it picked up and what are the factors that contribute to the mess? This was easy, too. One by one the reasons were suggested.

Supports

1. We each have our own room in which to keep our things.

2. We hire someone to clean once a week.

Barriers

1. Things are not put away right when we're done with them.

2. Sometimes there's an attitude of "it's not my job."

55

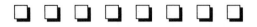

3. We don't have babies around anymore that keep their toys on the floor.
4. We have a cage to keep the dog in when we're not home.
5. There's plenty of storage space.

3. Too many toys.
4. No specific place to keep cassette tapes.
5. Magazines pile up waiting for us to have time to read them.
6. Things are left out at night and then they are the beginning of a mess the next day.
7. Dishes are often placed in the sink rather than directly in the dishwasher.
8. Clean clothes don't get put away in drawers when the laundry is folded.
9. We get home late and often feel rushed.
10. Having a cat and dog contributes to some of the mess.

To no one's surprise, the list of barriers was longer than the list of supports. From these lists, we developed an action plan and made some decisions about what steps we needed to take to reach our goal. This was a major event in our family to sit down as a "team" and decide on a common goal. Taking it through the steps of determining why it was important and what was keeping it in its current condition took us to the point of deciding what we were going to do about it. Without taking the time to do this, I'm sure the idea of keeping our house neat would have been a New Year's resolution wish rather than a family goal.

❏ *Your Challenge*

I know that I'm probably asking you to do something that is not a part of your everyday life at the current time. After all, some of us don't even have grocery lists when we go to the grocery store or have an idea about where we are going to be taking our next vacation. I can say that because it is very

□ □ □ □ □ □ □ □

familiar to me. I have found that in the areas of my life where I do not have specific goals, I don't accomplish what I'd really like to. I get sidetracked and I get busy, but I'm not always happy with the results of my activities. Setting goals is a way for me to focus my energies and to help me make decisions when daily choices crop up. Whether I should say "yes" or whether I should say "no" to requests becomes a matter of priorities and my being in control. If the request contributes to my goals, then the decision is easier to make. Likewise, when the request for my time does not contribute to my goals, I find it easier to say no when necessary. I challenge you to write down three to five goals in the areas of your life that you have determined are priorities. In the next chapter, we will be using these goals to develop an action plan. That's how to make these goals become a reality.

❑ *For Your Consideration:*

In what area of your life would you most like to see changes?

With what area of your life are you most satisfied?

What are the factors (supports) that keep the above areas of your life in their current condition?

What are the factors (barriers) that keep these areas of your life from changing?

❏ ❏ ❏ ❏ ❏ ❏ ❏ ❏

What was one instance where you kept focused on a goal despite hardships along the way?

Think of an area of your life in which your goals would have to be coordinated with someone else's goals.

6

The Action Plan:
Putting Good Intentions Into Daily Actions

Yvonne Prowant

"One of the purposes of the action plan is to get on track and stay there. Having an action plan will not automatically make the goal a reality. The real work in achieving goals is putting these actions into practice."

How does a goal change from something we desire to something we do? How do we change years of habits? Just knowing where you are and where you want to be is simply not enough to get you there. You need to develop a specific plan of action and then put that plan into practice. This is the next step in the accountability process.

This action plan will be very useful not only for your growth, but also for meeting with your accountability partner. It is these action steps and your completion of them that you will share back and forth when you meet. Your accountability partner will be there to give feedback on progress, make suggestions for other steps, and encourage you to take the steps you've outlined.

Developing the plan is not hard, but putting it into practice takes discipline. In this chapter I'll show you how to develop a plan to reach your specific goals and share some insight on how discipline can become a way of life.

Everyone is looking for instant changes — a quick fix. Our world is increasingly reinforcing this notion of instant action: FAX information, med stations, fast food, instant cash, and overnight deliveries. Time is becoming our most precious commodity and the quicker something can be done the better, or so it seems. Character development, however, is one area that cannot be rushed. In reality it takes time, energy, and sometimes significant events to discipline our actions and shape our characters. I think of it as being similar to the growth and development stages that we all progress through to reach a new level of maturity. We don't jump instantly from one stage to the next, for instance from crawling to walking, but develop slowly in an almost unseen process.

Have you ever had the feeling that when you reached a certain age or level of maturity that you wouldn't have to deal with the issues of "growing up" anymore? I did. When I was younger, I thought that when I reached adulthood I would attain some level of maturity at which the growth process would be complete. The problem was I didn't know what magical age that would be and I didn't know how to tell that I had arrived. Perhaps, I thought, it would happen with events such as college graduation, marriage, childbirth, or landing the right job. In reality, what I found was that these life-changing events only brought new areas of challenge for growth. At about age thirty- three, I began to realize that the process wasn't complete at all and in fact I couldn't foresee a time when I would know that I had stopped growing and had arrived at a level of maturity where I would want to stay.

The more I talk with others, the more I discover that I am not alone in this impression. I sense that most people think that the growth and development process "plateaus" when we reach adulthood until it declines as we approach our "old age." Actually, growth and development stages are now being identified for all adult years up to and including the death process.

Why does all that matter? I think it's important for us to realize that growth/development is a continual process. The challenge for us is to actively participate in our growth rather than just drift in the wind throughout our adulthood. When we have identified our values and have stated our goals, we know where we are headed. That's a major step many people fail to take. But even for those who do, most do not take their goals to the "next level" of writing down the specific steps necessary for achievement. This is called an action plan.

❏ *Write Your Plan*

An action plan is the step by step process which takes us from one place to another. It is dynamic in nature and highly individualized. Along the way, progress toward the goal is evaluated and changes are made as needed to achieve the goal.

The term "action plan" might sound like something requiring a lot of complicated work. Actually, developing the action plan is one of the easiest steps in the goal setting process. It might help to look at a few everyday examples of action plans and work through a couple of examples to see how to do it.

Many of us use actions plans on a daily basis without even realizing what they are. For example, when you get up in the morning, you might have a goal to be at work by eight a.m. There are a number of steps you take, rather automatically, to achieve that goal.

A recipe is another form of action plan. In this example, the goal is the end product, perhaps chocolate chip cookies. The time frame depends on whether you will mix the dough and refrigerate it or bake cookies today. The order of ingredients and the use of utensils are all identified in a step by step process. This step by step process is an action plan that takes you from a state of not having cookies to having some.

In the nursing profession, we have what are known as nursing care plans (action plans). Each starts with a goal for a particular patient that is based on a nursing assessment (like your personal assessment). Various steps are outlined to achieve that goal and are the directives for those who participate in the care. For example, included might be pain relief measures, teaching an aspect of self-care, or specific activity orders. On a regular basis, the patient's progress is evaluated. For some patients who are critical, this may occur every few minutes. For others in rehabilitation settings, it may be done weekly or monthly. The steps taken and the evaluation of progress are documented in the patient record. For those who are familiar with nursing, this constitutes a large part of the ever present "paperwork." Can you imagine a hospital stay with no common goal or consistent plan? Pain medication would be sporadic and dressing changes may or may not get done. People might lie in bed until the day of discharge if no one directed a gradual activity program!

❑ *Brainstorm*

Developing an action plan is simply brainstorming what steps could possibly be taken to achieve the goal and then selecting the ones you want to start putting into practice. According to the rules of brainstorming, you don't stop to evaluate ideas, you just write them down. Let's begin.

The place to start is the obvious. In the previous chapter on goals, you were asked to identify the supports and barriers to the achievement of a goal. Start your list of actions with these items. Jot down strategies that would either strengthen the supports or minimize the barriers. Don't stop now to evaluate. Just write them down.

After that, list all the other actions you can think of that could be used to reach the goal. Then look over the list. Now is the time to evaluate and select the ones that you think would work best for you. Be as specific as possible. For example, if you are going to exercise, describe the details. How? When? Where? With whom?

Work with one goal at a time. Don't limit yourself only to goals where you need to make improvement. There should be a balance of goals with which you are already successful and those upon which you need to improve. This is important for two reasons. First, you need to maintain those areas where you are successful. Identifying the steps that help you achieve that success will keep them on target and give you encouragement. We all like to hear positive comments. Also this affirmation lends balance to the goals in which we need improvement. Pastor Wayne refers to his list of goals as his "ten most wanted list." He balances this list both with goals at which he is successful and those at which he wants to improve. Few of us would be interested in doing this process if we felt overwhelmed by working only on all the areas in which we need improvement.

❑ *Try It!*

Step One: Take a sheet of paper and divide it in half or use the goal worksheet at the end of the chapter. If you are using a piece of paper, title one half "supports" and the other half "barriers." If you have already done this in the preceding chapter, proceed to step two. Then list all the supports and barriers you can think of that relate to this goal. List both the major and minor influences, both the ones that you think could easily be changed and ones that you see as an obstacle to success. This is a most interesting experience. Sometimes just doing this exercise helps us see why we're so

frustrated in some areas of our life. When the barriers far outweigh the supports, it is no wonder that we don't feel successful. It is from these two lists that you will begin to develop your action plan.

Step two: You are now ready to write down all the possible ways for you to achieve your goal. Again, don't spend a lot of time evaluating, just jot down ideas. This list could be quite long. Think about what could possibly be done to achieve the goal. Ask others what they think could be done. The options can range from simple — almost obvious — to complex. The more options you have, the more likely that you'll be able to choose the ones that will work for you. Start with the above two lists — capitalizing on supports and developing strategies to overcome barriers. In addition, create a list of other possible ways to achieve the goal.

Step three: From this list of possible ways for you to achieve your goal, pick the ones most likely to work and that you could realistically put into practice. Don't throw this list away though. As you begin your efforts and evaluate your progress along the way, you may want to add another step. Make the steps as specific as possible. You'll be more committed if you know exactly what you are to do. I challenge you to take this one step further and write your actions steps in your daily "to do" task lists. In doing this, these steps will be given appropriate priority and these actions will become a way of life.

❏ *Examples*

I have worked through two examples to illustrate this process. You'll notice in both that the steps are quite specific and individualized to my particular situation. Most people don't drink four bottles of pop a day. But for those who do, a fifty percent reduction would make a big difference. At two hundred calories each, that's eight hundred empty calories a day. 24,000 calories a month! A pound of fat is added every 3500 excess calories. If nothing else changes, I'll add seven pounds a month or eighty-four pounds a year just from this pop habit. Walking thirty minutes three times a week would do nothing for a marathon runner but would be a major step for someone who had not exercised at all. Running five miles a day would be a cinch for an avid runner, but impossible for a non-exerciser. You'll notice that my barriers far outweigh my supports. So that is why it's such a struggle!

In my example of my goal to get my payments to the creditors on time, I'd like to point out how the supports and barriers are the key to developing the right action steps and how simple the steps can be. The steps I outlined

are about as simple as can be and may seem like common sense. Even so, they were standing in the way of my money getting to the right place at the right time. This action plan was enough to change my behavior from a procrastinator with questionable credit to someone with responsible bill paying habits. Left unchecked, this habit could have led to a negative consequence. I think of how embarrassed I would have been if we were denied a mortgage because of a sloppy habit!! After all, the creditors don't care that I have enough money and just don't take the time to send it to them.

For someone who had a different set of supports and barriers, the action plan might look quite different. It may include getting a loan for debt consolidation, contacting creditors to set up a payment schedule or asking for a change in due date if all bills fall on the first of the month. Finding the right action steps to achieve a goal is like "locks and keys." The supports and barriers are the "locks." You can have a hundred solutions, like "keys," but if they don't fit the locks, they'll never open the door to goal achievement!

❑ Put It Into Practice!

Developing the action plan is only part of the process. One of the purposes of the action plan is to get on track and stay there. But it will not automatically make the goal a reality. The real work in achieving goals is putting these actions into practice. There are many days when we lose sight of our goals or when we just don't feel like doing what it takes. This is where discipline enters and discipline is the key to success.

The word discipline may bring to mind thoughts of punishment or reprimand. In this case, discipline is a self-directed control. M. Scott Peck, M.D., in his book *The Road Less Traveled* identifies discipline as the single most important tool in achieving life satisfaction. He further explains that discipline is made up of the following: delaying gratification, accepting responsibility, a dedication to reality and achieving a balanced life. He makes no promise that these steps will be fun, only that this discipline will lead to a successful life. The Bible also reminds us that discipline is not a "fun" process but one that is worth the effort. "No discipline seems pleasant at the time, but painful. Later on, however, it produces a harvest of righteousness and peace for those who have been trained by it" (Hebrews 12:11 NIV).

A poster hanging in my office shows a long stretch of road in an isolated countryside. A jogger in the foreground is heading toward a long uphill stretch. There are no other joggers or people in the scene. The caption

reads, "The race is not always to the swift, but to those who keep on running." It takes discipline to keep on running when you're the only one there. This is the benefit of having an accountability partner. He/she serves as a problem solver/encourager along the way as goals/action plans are reviewed regularly. When we might otherwise be alone, our accountability partner will be there.

In Hebrews 12:1-11, the writer speaks of discipline and shares an example from Jesus' life on earth:

"Therefore, since we are surrounded by such a great cloud of witnesses, let us throw off everything that hinders and the sin that so easily entangles, and let us run with perseverance the race marked out for us. Let us fix our eyes on Jesus, the author and perfector of our faith, who for the joy set before Him endured the cross, scorning its shame, and sat down at the right hand of the throne of God" (Hebrews 12:1-2, NIV).

❏ *A Lesson From Life*

The concept of action plans, discipline and human nature was probably best demonstrated to me one early Sunday morning in March. In fact, it was the morning that we were teaching about action plans in our accountability class. My husband had left early to serve as an usher. We live only one mile from the church, which started at 9:45. My plan was to leave by 9:30. At 9:25, my hunt for the car keys began. By 9:30, I realized that I was probably not going to find them and that I should look at my options. There were neighbors we could ride with — but they had already left. I could phone the church and ask Mick to come get us — but this was the time when the ushers were needed most. We could just skip. Our church averages two thousand people each Sunday. Who would notice? But, I was the teacher in our accountability class which started at 11:00. So our most reasonable option was to walk.

It was a beautiful morning, though a bit brisk. I knew the challenge would be to convince my nine-year-old daughter that she could make it and to keep my five-year-old son from dawdling too much along the way.

At approximately the "three-quarter mark," my daughter became discouraged. I had been through this before. It began with the verbal complaints and progressed to the "my will against your power" stage where she refused to take another step. Though reasoning didn't usually work, this time I had no other option.

My reasoning lesson that morning motivated her to continue walking,

but more than that it spoke to me about action plans. I first asked her to look back toward home. The stretch that we had walked had a gradual, slight incline. It looked like we had come a long way when we looked back. From where we stood, it looked like only a short city block to the church and we could see the drive. I explained that as I saw it she had three choices. One, turn around and go back home. It looked like a lot farther than what we had yet to go. Secondly, she could stay where she was. Time would still pass, people would pass her by, she would get cold and hungry, and eventually she would have to move in one direction or the other — or die. Or, she could continue, one step at a time in the direction of the church and perhaps take a rest along the way. If she chose the latter, it would not be long until she arrived at church.

My logic motivated her! She started moving, ever so slowly, one step at a time. More importantly, God used my lesson to teach me something. I'm amazed at how He uses my children to teach me spiritual truths. I've not forgotten that practical lesson about action plans. How often do I sit down somewhere between my starting point and my goal and face a struggle of the wills? How many times have I given up when if I would have taken just one step at a time, I would have made it? How many times have I sat down wherever I was, and others passed me by? It reminds me of a song which says, "just keep on walking, you don't know how far you've come, keep on walking . . . ." With an accountability partner, someone would be there at these points saying "Look how far you've come . . . You can do it!" or "As I see it, you have these choices."

❏ *It's Your Turn!*

I'm sure you're motivated by now to stop reading and start developing your own action plans so that you can achieve your goals. Let's review the entire process briefly:

1. Assess your personal situation.
2. Identify your values/priorities.
3. Set goals.
4. List the supports and barriers to achieving your goal.
5. Develop your action plan.
6. Put your action plan into practice.
7. Schedule your action steps in your calendar and on your daily tasks list.

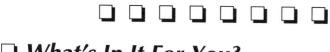

❏ *What's In It For You?*

Instant change it is not; but rather, a process for producing changes for long term growth. Action plans are a way for you to put structure and accountability into your goals and to change your good intentions into daily actions. It is the step by step process for how to get from a current condition to a desired one. Getting there will require discipline and determination. And an accountability partner is the encourager/motivator along the way to help you make progress.

❏ *For Your Consideration:*

1. What goal have you had that remains a wish because you don't have a specific plan to achieve it?

2. What good intentions have you had in the last month that never made their way into actions?

3. How can you overcome the barriers that stand in the way of achieving your goals?

4. Are you aware of what you're doing right in the areas of life in which you are successful?

5. How could the following help you in reaching your goal:

    Delaying gratification?
    Accepting responsibility?
        Looking at reality?
        Achieving balance?

7

Accountability In Five Dimensions: Spiritual

Wayne Schmidt

"The lifeline of a Christian's walk is his or her private times with God. There are no quick and easy substitutes for getting alone with our Heavenly Father."

It was one of life's most embarrassing moments. I was making a pastoral call at the hospital and had just finished my conversation with a patient recovering from major surgery. I stepped to her bedside in order to conclude our time together with prayer.

I bowed my head and began to pray fervently for her recovery. As I was concluding my prayer, the alarm on her IV machine began to sound. I ended my prayer rather abruptly, and opened my eyes to discover the reason for the alarm — I was standing on the tube!

We summoned the nurse, and both patient and nurse attempted to minimize my embarrassment by complaining how the lines are always becoming "twisted." While I appreciated their gracious attempts, they failed to halt the redness that was creeping up my neck toward my face. I left as quickly as I could!

After my bruised ego recovered to the point where I could laugh at myself, I also acknowledged that such an incident is a picture of the spiritual life of many people. In spite of their earnestness, they are blocking the very

lifelife necessary for their health!

The lifeline of a Christian's walk is his or her private times with God. There are no quick and easy substitutes for getting alone with our Heavenly Father. It is important to join publicly with other believers to worship, but that can never replace our individual times of worship. We may benefit from media ministers and messages, stimulating seminars and uplifting concerts — but in the long run, it will be the moments of solitude with our Sovereign Lord that provide the needed peace and power to cope and to hope.

But there's a problem with private times — they're private! The proving of our integrity most often occurs in the realm of the private — our secret thoughts, motives, and fears. Those things no one else shares with us are the things most easily left undone. One goal of accountability is to make the private dimensions of life more open and known — to an individual or group we can trust.

Let's be "up front" with one another — the one feeling many of us associate with personal devotions is guilt — guilt for the days we skipped, the times we were so tired that we fell asleep as we prayed, the moments our minds wandered. Before entering the ministry, I hoped that as a pastor these problems would miraculously disappear when I was ordained. Guess what — I experience the same challenges, and maybe even greater feelings of failure and guilt!

Through God's grace and my accountability, my devotional life has grown. Significant interaction with my Heavenly Father still does not come automatically — and I suspect that's true for even the most pious of saints. As with any worthwhile relationship, along with the joy and spontaneity come discipline and hard work.

❏ *Values Set The Vision*

We don't have personal devotional times because we "feel like it." Left to "feelings," personal devotions will at best be a hit-and-miss business. We regularly commune with God because we value our relationship with Him — and what we value sets the vision for what can and should take place.

It is good to put values and priorities into action. What is the goal of accountability? It is to ensure that we are more than hearers of God's Word — we are doers. So what takes place in our devotional life begins with our values — a sense of conviction of what is important to us, and as Christians,

what is important to God.

A frequently quoted verse is found in Proverbs 29:18 "Without vision, the people perish." The New International Version translates it "Where there is no revelation, the people cast off restraint." If we are to restrain (discipline) ourselves, we need a vision that springs from our values.

I've noticed the impact of values in the church where I serve as pastor. From the beginning, our philosophy of ministry has identified three core values:

Adoration - we exist to worship Jesus Christ and submit to His lordship.

Acceptance - we meet people on the basis of their needs as individuals, not by judging whether they meet our needs as a church. We affirm the value of each person as a creation of God and object of His redemptive work.

Accountability - while we do not expect people to come to us complete (acceptance!), we do expect them to join us in the process of being created anew by God.

These values shape the vision of our church, and provide a framework through which all ministry directions are filtered. They create the "atmosphere" for our ministry.

In the same way, what I individually value helps establish the internal atmosphere of my life. The same is true for you. What is it that you value in your relationship with God? How would you characterize your private times with God if they were going exactly as you wished?

It's helpful to state values positively. Picture them as if they were already taking place. Let me share with you my values for the spiritual dimension of my life:

❑ I have a growing, personal relationship with God made possible by God's Son and Spirit.

❑ I have open communication with God through consistent prayer times.

❑ I desire to reflect on God's will for who I am as a person and what I'm to do as His servant.

❑ I am deepening my knowledge of and commitment to God and His will through the study of His Word.

Are all of these true every day? Not always! But they formulate my vision for what I value in my personal relationship with Christ. They are a picture of my longings, and give focus to the goals I establish for my devotional life.

❏ *Goals Guide Growth!*

Exercises of the private spiritual life have often been referred to as the "disciplines." Most of us would agree that a growing relationship with Christ requires a substantial amount of discipline. But the goal is not to be disciplined, to read Scripture, to pray — these are the means to a higher end. What we seek to develop is vibrant personal interaction with God.

The danger with "disciplines" is that we tend to become legalistic or compulsive about their performance. The result is a disconnection of the outward practice from the inward purpose. Oh, I may read my chapter of the Bible every day, and so compulsively fill my "quota." The real test is this — have I read it with my heart and mind open to God's Spirit to apply it in my life?

There are certain basic commitments that contribute to building a relationship with God. Identifying them is not a guessing game — they are revealed for us in the Scriptures.

❏ *The Practice Of Prayer*

How mind-boggling — to think that God has made it possible for me as a limited creature to interact with Him as the unlimited, holy Creator. It is not only possible, but He loves to spend time in communication with those who belong to Him!

How tragic that for many believers prayer has become a mindless, unreflective practice — little more than rote recital of phrases that have been used for years by the person praying or by others. How easily the focus moves from the attitude of worship to the appropriate articulation of words. God is not impressed with eloquence but with the earnestness (sincerity) of the seeker.

Let's take a moment to look at some misconceptions about prayer. First of all, prayer is not giving God information, but interacting with Him. God knows all — my victories, my disappointments, my temptations, my desires. I do not need to tell Him about my schedule or circumstances so that He won't be left in the dark. He wants me to bring these things to Him not for the purpose of His awareness, but my awareness. Talking about the events of life with God serves as a reminder that He cares and has a purpose in my daily activities and challenges. I must become "tuned in" to His perspective.

Nor is prayer an opportunity to moan, groan, and complain. There is a close resemblance between the voice of some adults while praying and the voice of some children while whining! Whining irritates others and at times must irritate God. With my children, a request made in a whining voice goes unanswered — and often they would get what they were seeking had they used a normal tone of voice! It is appropriate to honestly express our needs and problems — God wants us to bring those to Him. But they should be offered in the context of gratitude for the deep joy and security that belong to us in Christ.

Prayer is not a time to "worry out loud." Many people who through prayer seek to leave their anxieties "at the altar" take them away when they leave. One definition of worry is "taking responsibility for things we can neither change or control." So prayer is a time of sorting out responsibility — determining God's will for what I can change or control, and then in an act of faith leaving the rest with Him. It is then we fulfill Philippians 4:6:

> *"Do not be anxious about anything, but in everything, by prayer and petition, with thanksgiving, present your request to God."*

This verse is a command, not an option. God never gives us more than we can handle (1 Corinthians 10:13) — but often we foolishly take on more than He gives!

Prayer is a time of two-way communication with God. We talk and we listen. It is communion. It is an awareness of His presence in us and in the world. It is an opportunity to refine our perspectives and realign ourselves with His will.

I live in Michigan which has been labeled the "Winter Wonderland" state. One of the side effects of our glorious winter is the break-down of our road system, leaving numerous potholes. These roads wreak havoc on the wheel alignment of our cars, causing additional wear and tear as well as difficulty steering our cars in their intended direction.

You and I need alignment too — when the "potholes" of life jar us. Prayer serves to realign us with our Creator, sparing us unnecessary wear and tear. Just as poor alignment causes a car to wander, so when we are poorly aligned spiritually we tend to wander from the path God has designed for us. "Prone to wander, Lord, I feel it, prone to leave the God I love."

❏ *When We Pray*

How often we pray can be guided by how often we desire to communicate with anyone we love. Many Christians pray daily, others every day except weekends, and some once or twice a week.

People who are more "structured" like to pray at the same time every day while others vary their schedule of prayer.

The time of day also is a matter of personal preference. The best time is when we are most alert and freed from distractions. When it came to prayer, David seemed to be a "morning person":

> *"Morning by morning, O Lord, you hear my voice;*
> *Morning by morning I lay my requests before you*
> *and wait in expectation" (Psalm 5:3).*

I wholeheartedly agree with David — I'm alert in the morning. My mind is not yet preoccupied with the concerns of the day, and prayer sets the tone for the hours ahead. Although it's beyond my comprehension, there are rumored to be people for whom morning is not the best time. "Early" is anything before lunch, brain cells aren't stimulated until hours after that first cup of coffee, and they consider "morning people" to be a nuisance. At ten o'clock at night (bedtime for us normal people) they're just getting wound up, and midnight is "prime time." The best time for them to pray is not before others get up, but after others go to bed!

❏ *Where To Pray*

Some would argue that it doesn't matter where we pray. God is everywhere. He no longer dwells in buildings or rooms, but He takes up residence in those who belong to Him. We can talk with Him at home, at church, or while walking in the woods. He is certain to be attentive to us at anytime and in any place.

While having a regular place does not benefit God, it can certainly benefit us. It can become a special sanctuary for us — a "prayer closet." A "prayer closet" can be a favorite chair, a particular room in the house, or any place that becomes a familiar place to meet with God.

I can remember while still a boy getting up early and seeing my dad

having his personal devotional time. He always sat leaning against the wall heater — a warm place in early mornings. Recently I had lunch with a businessman who prays while riding his exercise bike. I prefer my office which has a beautiful view of a large woods. Another friend has a favorite stool that she always kneels beside.

The same criteria that determine the best time also help us locate the best place. It is the place where we will be most alert and freed from distractions.

❏ *How To Pray*

While growing up, I suffered from the "slumping shoulder syndrome" — more popularly known as poor posture. My parents and other concerned adults constantly prodded me to exercise proper posture. Is there a proper posture for prayer? Should we stand, sit, kneel, lie, walk, or, like the friend I mentioned earlier, ride an exercise bike?

While a familiar posture may aid a person much like a familiar place, I believe it's best to let the posture fit the mood. That means when I'm humbling myself before God, I may lie face down. When I'm repenting of some sin, I may kneel. When I'm rejoicing, I may stand with hands raised. When I'm just discussing matters with the Lord, I may be seated.

Often when I pray, I walk. Walking keeps me alert and relaxed. When I pray for church staff members with whom God has given me the opportunity to serve, I will often stand outside their office doors. Since it is early morning, no one is there — and standing outside their doors helps me focus on their lives and needs.

❏ *What To Pray*

If prayer is a conversation with God, what should the conversation cover? The simplest response is "whatever is on a person's heart or mind." A format, however, can help guide our interaction with God.

One of the most popular is the widely used A-C-T-S format. It goes as follows:

A - Adoration. Begin with praise for who God is and what He has done. The goal is to exalt God and humble oneself.

C - Confession. Identify any sin or disobedience that may be hindering

fellowship with God. Repentance is offered and cleansing is requested.

T - Thanksgiving. Express gratitude to God for His blessings personally and for prayers He has answered.

S - Supplication. Make requests to God for the needs of the world, church, country, family, and personal life.

Note the basic elements of prayer — praise, confession, seeking God's provision and direction. These dimensions are found in the prayers of David (Psalm 5), Nehemiah (Nehemiah 1:5-11), and the Disciple's Prayer (Matthew 6:9-13). Organize them in a way that serves as a catalyst for your conversation with God.

One of my favorite pictures hangs on a wall in my office. I received it as a gift early in my ministry. It is a picture of a person sitting across a desk from Christ. It is obvious that Christ is quietly discussing this person's needs and giving direction. I often contemplate that scene before I pray. It provides a valuable reminder that a growing relationship with Christ is nurtured by regular times of seeking His perspective on life.

❑ *Get Into God's Word*

The second crucial ingredient of devotional life is the reading of God's Word. When practiced with prayer, the results are life-changing. Prayer illumines our understanding of God's Word. God's Word provides us with the raw material of revelation which the Holy Spirit applies to our lives to create a finished product.

When reading God's Word, we are not simply seeking information. Such reading is not advance preparation for our next game of "Bible trivia." We are not computers seeking to build our data base. While we may gain a greater grasp of biblical facts, knowledge for knowledge's sake is a dangerous commodity.

> *"Knowledge puffs up, but love builds up. The man who thinks he knows something does not yet know as he ought to know" (1 Corinthians 9:1-2).*

Our goal is application of God's Word to our lives. Remember, that is also the goal of accountability — that the principles of Scripture become ingrained in our lives.

"Do not merely listen to the word, and so deceive yourselves. Do what it says. Anyone who listens to the word but does not do what it says is like a man who looks at his face in a mirror and, after looking at himself, goes away and immediately forgets what he looks like. But the man who looks intently into the perfect law that gives freedom, and continues to do this, not forgetting what he has heard, but doing it — he will be blessed in what he does" (James 1:22-25 NIV).

As we read God's Word, we must constantly be attentive to the whispers of the Holy Spirit, who helps us integrate God's truth into daily life.

Our Bible reading goal is personal development. It is not a time to gather ammunition to defend our latest theological passion. It is not preparation time for a sermon or lesson. It is not a time to see how God's Word applies to someone else — it is a time to apply His Word.

Many people utilize devotional guides such as "The Upper Room" or "Light From the Word" while reading Scripture. These can be helpful supplements to reading God's Word, but never substitutes. Many people are also guided in their reading by "schedules" that are available from a variety of sources. I personally follow a schedule that includes passages from the Old Testament, New Testament, Psalms, and Proverbs for each day of the year, and which allows me to read through the entire Bible in a year. The reading requires of me ten minutes each day, and I'm beginning to sense the rich rewards that come from "multiple journeys" through the Bible!

A yellow light of caution — when you're accountable to read God's Word, it is tempting to skim through so you can check the goal off your list. If you do so, your interaction with God's Word will be superficial. Don't be in such a hurry to fulfill the immediate requirement that you miss the long term benefits that come from thoughtful contemplation and application of God's Word to your life!

❏ *Keep A Journal*

For years I've prayed and read God's Word, but only in the last few years have I entered into a new discipline — keeping a journal.

Journaling wars against my natural inclination, which is why I need to do it. I'm a person who parrots the cliche "What's past is past." I view looking back as a waste of time, and rarely celebrate or commiserate over what took place yesterday. Yet there is a problem with that approach to life.

It results in a failure to learn all we can, and makes us vulnerable to repeating the errors of the past.

Keeping a journal forces me to reflect. I picture myself taking notes from God. Since I make entries in my journal following my prayer time, I try to see myself recording God's perspective on the activities of my life — how I've related to people, performed my ministry, disciplined my thoughts and resisted temptation.

Each time I write I usually cover an 8 1/2 x 11 page. If I try to write more, I grow weary. On one "half sheet" I take "A Look Back" at my life's events since I last made a journal entry. On the other half I look ahead and try to anticipate a godly response in future decisions and situations. Among my journal entries:

> ❏ did I have the proper attitude and use the proper approach in confronting a friend?
> ❏ how should I respond to people who leave our local church because "it doesn't meet their needs"?
> ❏ what might God's will be for decisions at a coming meeting?
> ❏ how'm I doing in emotionally and spiritually nurturing my wife and children?

I resist the pressure to try to make all my entries profound. I'm not trying to impress myself or God, and no one else reads my journal anyway. Journaling provides a wonderful opportunity for reflection.

❏ *How To Get Started*

In addition to prayer, Bible reading and journaling, there are other disciplines conducive to spiritual growth. These include (but are not limited to) fasting, solitude, and simplicity through self-denial. Don't try them all at once! If you're starting from scratch, perhaps begin with Bible Study and prayer. After those are going well, you can then add journaling, fasting, or some other form of discipline.

One of my favorite gifts at Christmas is a box of chocolate "samplers." It contains a variety of chocolate delights from which I have the opportunity to choose. In each of the following chapters on specific areas of accountability, we will be offering to you an "accountability sampler" of potential goals. Choose the one or ones that represent a reasonable step of growth for you in your private devotional life:

❑ ❑ ❑ ❑ ❑ ❑ ❑ ❑

❑ I will pray ten minutes a day using the A-C-T-S format
    as a guideline.
❑ I will read through the Bible during the next 365 days.
❑ I will pray for at least one hour each week at three or four
    different times.
❑ I will make a journal entry twice a week.
❑ I will read the Bible for ten minutes at least five
    days every week.
❑ I will fast one meal each month and spend that time in
    prayer.

The possibilities are limitless. It's best to set a goal that challenges you but does not overwhelm you.

❑ *Today's "Higher Revving Engines"*

A television commercial displays the inward workings of an engine being driven at a high rate of speed. The effects are dramatic when the oil breaks down and the friction of metal on metal begins. Then the engine itself shuts down. The caption is :

"With today's higher revving engines, you need _____ motor oil."

Most people I know have "higher revving engines" — in other words, the hectic demands of schedule, the needs of family, the requirements of career "rev" their internal motors. It is easy to overlook the need for the "lubrication" of God's Spirit through personal devotions. It takes discipline and accountability — a partner or partners asking us if these times with God are really happening, and what we're learning because of them.

The natural tendency of any relationship, most particularly our relationship with God, is to "float to the surface" — to become shallow or superficial. That's the reason at least two of my "Top Ten" goals every year relate to personal devotions. Even though I meet my goals regularly, I feel that without accountability, the risks of hypocrisy dramatically escalate.

Think of the possibilities — God's Spirit working in and through me. If Michelangelo were within me, I could create fantastic sculptures. If Luciano Pavorotti indwelt me, I could amaze audiences with my musical capabilities.

If Albert Einstein lived within me, I could grasp and articulate the complexities of physics. As a Christian, the limitless Christ dwells in me!

"He is the image of the invisible God, the firstborn over all creation. For by him all things were created: things in heaven and on earth, visible and invisible, whether thrones or powers or rulers or authorities; all things were created by him and for him. And he is the head of the body, and in him all things hold together" (Colossians 1:15-17).

Our private devotional times open us to Christ's dwelling richly and powerfully in our lives.

Remember my embarrassing moment with that I-V alarm? Yvonne has lessened my chagrin by informing me that those alarms are simply there to alert the nurse early in order to avoid major problems like clogged tubing or disconnection from the patient. Sometimes the alarms in our private lives signal us "early on" to potential danger. Don't wait, my friend! Act now to keep your spiritual lifeline open!

This area of life is too important to "go it alone." Accountability will keep you pursuing the spiritual disciplines when your determination begins to falter. Accountability to another only enhances our accountability to God!

❏ *For Your Consideration:*

What are the reasons that many people struggle with regular personal devotions — quiet times of prayer and scripture study?

What is it you value in your relationship with God? How would you characterize your private times with God if they were going exactly as you wished?

How long?

What would they include?

❏ ❏ ❏ ❏ ❏ ❏ ❏ ❏

How would you feel because of them?

If you were to describe the practice of prayer to someone who had never prayed before, what would you tell them?

Prayer is not...

Prayer is...

Philippians 4:6: How does prayer help us combat worry?

Psalm 119:11 tells us "Your Word have I hid in my heart, that I might not sin against you." How does reading and reflecting upon God's Word prevent sin?

❏ *Time to ACT:*

My goals for personal devotional life are:

8

Accountability In Five Dimensions: Family

Wayne Schmidt

"All happy families resemble one another; every unhappy family is unhappy in its own way" (Leo Tolstoy).

"God's Word is specific — the integrity of our spiritual lives should first be evident to those who live with us and know us best."

Family life in America is experiencing changes of epidemic proportions. The image most of us carry in our minds of the so-called "typical family" no longer squares with reality. The so-called traditional family unit of father as bread-winner and mother who stays home to care for two or more children is now a minority image at best. U.S. census statistics tell us that while in 1960 such a unit constituted 60% of American households, it currently represents less than 10%. The impact among other things comes from our aging population, the number of two-career households, an escalating divorce rate, and young people waiting longer to marry.

I've witnessed the changes in our church congregation. Half of all first-time visitors are single. A ministry to divorced individuals involves hundreds. Children are in church every other week because they divide their weekends between divorced parents. Our Child Care Center has experienced explosive growth because of the number of working mothers.

We've adjusted our ministry approaches because we recognize:

❏ Half of all children under sixteen will see their parents divorce, and half of all children in America will have lived in a single-parent household.

❏ The number of single parent families has doubled in the past ten years.

❏ Of those who divorce, 80% will remarry within three years.

Greater sensitivity than ever before is needed when speaking of "God's desires for family life."

It is impossible in one chapter to take into account all of the unique family situations of those who will read these words. No matter what our family structure, however, God has called us to demonstrate the character of Christ in our home setting.

❏ *Values Set The Vision*

God's Word is specific — the integrity of our spiritual lives should first be evident to those who live with us and know us best. The Apostle Paul, when selecting spiritual leaders, made it clear that leadership begins at home: "If anyone does not manage his own family, how can he take care of God's church?" (1 Timothy 3:5). Christ compared His relationship with the church to the marriage relationship of the home (Ephesians 5:22-33).

Who determines our model for how a family should interact? Some people look to the media and the result is greater confusion than ever! A television station in our area carries old reruns of "Leave It To Beaver." Family interaction is orderly, predictable, respectful, and overly idealistic. The same station carries the latest editions of "The Simpsons" — disorderly, sarcastic, self-loathing, and hopefully not realistic! Who should function as a family role model — Beaver Cleaver or Bart Simpson?

Other people may look to their friends or neighbors in trying to determine norms of family living. That also can lead to confusion. For instance, when I want to determine who should mow the lawn, I like to look at our neighbors to the east. In that family, the wife mows the lawn. My wife, Jan, likes to look to the neighbors to the west. In that family the husband mows the lawn. Which is proper?

A sense of family is important regardless of the form that family takes. Many factors enter into this sense of family, more than simply being related to one another. In November 1990, our local paper, *The Grand Rapids Press*, published a tribute to families. In that they highlighted various families, some looking quite non-traditional and identified the exceptional ties that held them together. Overall they identified the following ingredients

that the family bond was built with: compassion, love, sharing, and caring.

Chuck Swindoll in his book *Growing Wise in Family Life* reports on a research project by Dr. Nick Stinnett, chairman of the Department of Human Development and the Family at the University of Nebraska. This project observed families in several countries. They did not limit their research to Christian or traditional families. The one criterion for inclusion was a high rating in marriage happiness and satisfaction in parent-child relationships. They identified the following as desired qualities for a "strong" family:

1) members are committed to the family
2) they spend time together
3) they have good family communication
4) they express appreciation to each other
5) they have a spiritual commitment
6) they are able to solve problems in a crisis

All of us have had our family life values shaped by our family of origin. Some of us delight in those memories and some of us attempt to block them out. It may be an example of either what we want to embrace or want to avoid. More than ever, we are understanding that our past impacts our present.

Dysfunctional family systems have distorted or clouded many people's vision of the family. An angry young lady vows to never be like her mother, yet the behavioral resemblances are striking. An adult child of an alcoholic struggles to overcome the shame and feeling of abandonment in order to have an intimate marriage relationship. A father struggles with overpowering anger that has roots in his abusive childhood.

There is great danger as adults in structuring our present or future family life in reaction to our family of origin. It is the "pendulum effect." Because a person was raised under strict discipline, he or she may be overly lenient with his or her own children. Due to open conflict between a person's parents, an overreaction is the suppression of differences and perceived needs to "keep the peace." The pendulum swings to one extreme for a certain generation, then back to the other extreme for the next generation. It is one way in which the sin of the fathers carries on down to the third and fourth generation (Exodus 20:5). In such cases, a healthy balance is never achieved.

God's Word must guide us in establishing family values — whether married or single, parent or child, in a first marriage or remarriage, we must live consistently with God's revealed will. That means we demonstrate the character of Christ and give energy to the commitments that foster enduring and enriching relationships.

Such a determination requires sensitivity to the Holy Spirit. A single-parent with numerous demands on time needs to seek God's guidance as to

how best to invest in his or her children. A married couple should seek God's will as to how to build an intimate, meaningful marriage. A teen needs to experience God's prompting as how to best honor his or her parents.

❏ *Our Values*

Let me share my values for the family dimension of life. My wife and I currently have two sons, although we're exploring the possibility of adopting a daughter. Values are, you remember, a positive statement of how you would desire life to be, and are phrased as if they are present reality:

❏ I am growing in my love and commitment to my wife and children.

❏ I am providing time in my calendar to allow family communication to go beneath the surface to the real and significant issues of life.

❏ I am praying for my wife and children on a consistent basis, seeking God's will and insight for their well-being and growth.

❏ Next to my relationship with God, the most important relationship I have is with my wife.

❏ I am building a relationship with my children as, first of all, their dad, but, as a close second, their friend and "cheerleader."

It's obvious that my values reflect the formulation of my family system. Your values should do the same, and so may be different from mine. One thing, however, should be constant. God's Word and God's Spirit should be the highest and strongest forces in the forging of any family's values.

❏ *Goals To Guide Growth*

Family life is one area where there is much more said than done. Other pressing demands squeeze out the less urgent needs of a spouse or child. For many it is not until their family unit disintegrates that family life is given the attention it needs. Then it's a case of "too little, too late" or people realize after the children are grown what should have been done.

Goals should contribute to the values we hold, helping us to practice what we profess. If married, we should have goals that support and strengthen our marriage. If parents, how can our relationship with our child be more than peaceful co-existence? As a member of an extended family, what is my role and responsibility? If you are in a dating relationship or

86

seriously anticipating marriage, what is the standard by which you will be guided?

❏ *Marriage: A Mutual Ministry!*

Marriage is a commitment of love and faith. It is a commitment of mutual ministry. It is in the context of relationships that we learn most about ourselves and others. Marriage is not only to satisfy us but to stretch us. There is probably no other relationship which calls for a deeper commitment to Christlike character.

As a pastor, I've performed weddings for hundreds of people. I've spent hours in premarital and marital counseling. I'm convinced marriage relationships move through certain phases.

The first phase I'll call "Mutual Enjoyment." This is the honeymoon stage which lasts from a few minutes to a few months. The couple is certain they could never be more in love! Expectations are fulfilled and those unmet seem to make little difference. If the toast is burnt, hey, that's okay — it's best a little crunchy anyway!

The next phase is that of "Mutual Adjustment." It's now obvious that expectations (unrealistic or realistic) aren't being met. The couple wonders at times whether they're in love. The discovery is made that marriage is work. Many exit the relationship due to "incompatibility" rather than investing the energy and flexibility needed in all great relationships. If the toast is burnt, the reaction is either a verbal bashing or the "silent treatment."

What people do with this gap between expectations and reality determines the future of the marriage. Many long term marriages are still stuck at this point! Though they can boast many years of marriage, they have not progressed to the next step.

The final phase is one of "Mutual Fulfillment." If the first phase is marked by idealism, and the second by pessimism, then this phase is marked by optimistic realism. Love tempered by time and commitment has grown deep. A compatibility and comfort emerges. You make your own toast the way you like it!

My marriage has moved through those phases. It has taken practical commitments for which I am accountable to help it mature. One of those commitments is to "date" my wife. Those dates that built our relationship leading up to marriage are necessary to continue building it today.

Our goal is to date at least once every two weeks. We must be alone together — not with our children or with another couple. We should be in a setting conducive to conversation — so that we can talk honestly and

lovingly about how we're doing individually and as a couple. It's a time to express our love for one another and give encouragement to help each other grow.

Often our dates are not elaborate — some of the simplest have been the best. It may be a walk holding hands, a bike ride to the yogurt shop, a trip to a park — anywhere that allows us to catch up on each other's lives and stay in touch with each other's feelings. That is "what works."

A few years back, my wife Jan and I attended a seminar in which the leader (a successful pastor) "opened up." He told of how his wife had confronted him with the fact he had a mistress. After he adamantly denied it, she clarified what she meant. The church he pastored was his "mistress" — it received his best spiritual, mental and emotional energy. She felt jilted, rejected.

When we walked out of that seminar, I asked Jan if she had ever experienced those feelings. I anticipated her answer — yes. Though not true now, she explained, it was true in the early years of our marriage and ministry. One of the commitments that turned things around was our "dates" together — dates that happen because they're a priority — and I'm accountable for them!

There have been weeks in which I failed to make time for a date. It was not a lack of desire — it was a lack of discipline. I knew my accountability meeting was coming, and I hadn't met that goal. I'd quickly ask my wife for a date!

The marriage is the primary relationship of the home, and no other relationship should receive higher priority with the exception of our relationship with God. Some people attempt to substitute other relationships and give it the primary place. I'm not talking just of adulterous relationships, but relationships otherwise wholesome — except that they are placed above marriage. That includes even our children. Unwilling to make the adjustments of marriage and expend the emotional energy required, couples may be tempted to focus on the children. Children are neither capable nor deserving of taking a place of priority above marriage! Kids are adversely affected when emotionally pressured to become the "substitute" spouse in order to compensate for a marriage suffering from not-so-benign neglect.

Years ago a wise pastor informed me that the greatest gift I can give my children is a healthy and loving marriage with their mom. When the marriage functions as God designed it, there comes to the total home a sense of peace and security.

My accountability partner some years ago began a practice that has been an example to me. A successful businessman, he has long recognized the value of annual planning in corporate settings. These are times to evaluate

the past, identifying strengths and weaknesses present in the company. These are times to try to anticipate the future and what is needed to build a strong, growing enterprise.

This man has taken that simple concept and applied it to his marriage. Each year he and his wife get away for a few days of "annual planning." They pick a setting that is conducive to relaxation as well as discussion. They talk about all aspects of their relationship, including finances, ministry opportunities, potential vacations, friendships with others, and their spiritual lives. It's a time to identify strengths and weaknesses that are present and to strategize how to build a strong, growing, lasting marriage.

My wife and I have tried an annual planning time just once now. It was tough! Our long list of items on the "agenda" didn't get covered. The rewards of being together, however, and making that investment in our relationship were evident.

If you're married, have you ever thought about asking your husband/wife this question: What are the two or three things that are most important to you? So often we function from what we assume from our past or what the media dishes out. One person may value regular home-cooked meals while another may value "advance warning" if company is invited. It is important to find out what matters to them. What is needed to nurture your relationship toward its God-given possibilities? It may be regular dating, an annual retreat, and/or other investments of time and energy. Maybe it's as simple as communicating each other's schedules. Do you and your spouse ever feel like two ships who pass in the night? One thing is certain — great marriages don't just "happen." Just as a garden requires cultivation to bring forth a harvest, so a marriage requires cultivation and attention to bring a blessing to each other and to give glory to God.

❏ *The Power of Parenting*

Kids have a way of rearranging life. Couples who felt like experts on parenting before having children feel incompetent once they come! As one new mother said of her children: "I've certainly made my mistakes — my children didn't come with an owner's manual."

The challenging thing about raising children is the continual change! When my first son was born, I felt bad that we had to learn to parent as he grew. He was our "guinea pig" who endured our early attempts and experiments with parenting. We learned a lot, and I knew when our other children came along, we'd have our act together!

Our second son was born — and suddenly all the rules changed! He was drastically different from our first-born — in personality, in behavior, and in response to us. I could hardly believe that two children so different from one another sprang from the same set of parents!

Not only are there challenges related to birth order, but to the ages and stages of maturity. I hear parents lament the fact their pre-schoolers require more energy than they can give. I also hear moms and dads talk about "surviving" the teen years of their children, viewing it as a marathon of endurance and patience. I also hear parents bemoaning the coming "empty nest" and the struggles of helping children establish new and independent lives. Whatever age the children, there are challenges!

Is it any wonder then, that Scripture calls on us to be sensitive to our children and their needs — to be tuned in to their constant changes? As one wise person put it:

"Train a child in the way he should go, and when he is old he will not turn from it" (Proverbs 22:6 NIV).

That verse is commanding parents to discipline and develop their children in a way that is appropriate to their individual needs — needs that are unique to each child and changing as they mature.

No matter what age your children are, communication is of utmost importance. Though it will take many forms as the child matures, it should start in infancy. Most parents do this naturally. Have you ever noticed mothers talking to babies and toddlers in the grocery cart? When does communication break down? There is no magical age. It happens whenever one party stops talking or one party stops listening.

Many people ignore kids and don't think that what they have to say is of much value. I always respect a person who takes the time to listen to and respond to a child's question or comment rather than just offering an absent-minded "uh huh", "uh huh." In 1988, a task force at our local church looked at children's needs in the face of our changing families and how we as a local church could effectively minister to children. One comment from a social worker stands out, "Self esteem cannot be taught. It is the result of being known, loved, and accepted." This requires time and energy.

Many parents said they didn't know how to talk to or how to play with their children. Thirty-two percent of children at Kentwood Community Church said they didn't have time alone with their dads, and nineteen percent said they didn't have time alone with their moms. Many parents and children confessed to hectic schedules that contributed to a "stressed-out," uncommunicative environment.

Yvonne shares that she and Mick have held weekly "family calendar meetings" for the last three years and has found this is an important

communication avenue. Each family member reviews his/her schedule for the coming week (including the six-year-old who might report which day is gym day or if he's going to a birthday party). They then take a week overview. If there is a night with nothing scheduled, that's a good time to make a family decision about what to do. It has brought to reality those comments of "maybe someday we'll do . . . ." If there is something scheduled for every day, it's a good time to rethink if all those activities are important and cancel the ones that aren't. It has eliminated their making assumptions about Yvonne counting on Mick (or vice-versa) to get the kids off to school for a particular day only to find out the night before that there was a conflict. They have taken this one step further to plan vacations or special days away from home for the upcoming three months.

My sons are currently in their elementary school years. One of the ways I've attempted to stay in touch with their world these past few years is to enter into it through play times. Three times a week we play together, and they choose what we play. They've chosen soccer, sledding, basketball, baseball, wrestling and other fairly normal activities. They've also been creative — designing games like "Under the Blanket." It's pretty simple — dad gets on the floor under a blanket, and they run and jump on him!

They love playing with dad. They love beating up on him! They even pray they will be the victors in our wrestling matches. That presents me with a real dilemma — do I want them to believe God answers prayer and get beat up, or do I want to win?

I'm realistic. Our play times will never make them great basketball players or wrestlers. I do hope they will know their dad loves them and enjoys being part of their lives. I'm accountable for these regular play times, and will set aside tiredness or personal preference to meet this goal.

Goals will change as they grow. We're discovering as parents that we need to spend more time with our sons individually. We're planning to establish "dates" where each of us as parents takes a child out for something special on a monthly basis. As they enter the early teen years, I desire to spend some intensive time in discipleship with each child.

Are these goals established because I love them? Certainly! But there's much more. God has entrusted these children to me for a time. He has "loaned" these kids who belong to Him, and has given me the responsibility for and stewardship of their development. Then they will be prepared to establish a meaningful relationship with their true and eternal Parent — their Heavenly Father.

❑ *Other Family Relationships*

There are many other family relationships that could be included in accountability goals. It could be goals to demonstrate respect for parents. It might be ways to establish closer ties with siblings. It may be someone in the extended family — grandparents, aunts and uncles, cousins — who could benefit from an investment of our time and energy. It might involve appropriate limit setting with parents who've never let you become an independent adult. It may be setting standards in the context of dating or choosing a mate and asking someone to hold you accountable for those standards.

With changing family structures, this goal setting becomes more complex. Many children relate not only to their biological parents but to step-parents. Many households are now a combination of "yours, mine, and ours" — the special needs of a blended family. One of the classes in our church's adult education program zeroes in on equipping parents in the blended family because it is such a real, pressing need.

What are some measurable, specific goals that can be set for the family dimension? The following are simply samples and suggestions offered as starting points in setting your own:

❑ I will date my spouse at least once every two weeks, getting alone for conversation about the significant and lasting issues of life.

❑ I will pray for my family at least three times a week.

❑ I will spend some individual time with each of my children at least once a week.

❑ I will pray with my spouse at least once a week.

❑ I will visit my grandparent in the nursing home at least once each month and at holiday times.

❑ I will write to _____ at least twice each month.

❑ I will get a special surprise (card, gift, etc.) at least once every two weeks for my spouse.

There are many possibilities for goals. First choose the relationships you want or feel called to develop. Then set goals representing practical actions that will contribute to the building up of that person and relationship.

My wife and I are considering enlarging our family through adoption. As part of the process, we had to undergo a thorough home study. It helped us identify anew and afresh strengths as well as needed areas of growth in our family. A growing family is a lifelong commitment.

It also was a time to reflect upon how much we value our family and to

□ □ □ □ □ □ □ □

ask the tough question: Is that family value evidenced in our budget, our calendar, and our decisions? We want to be certain that it is, and that's the goal of accountability — vision becoming reality!

Now is the time for you to put your good intentions for family relationships into action. Seize the opportunities that today offers — and begin building for tomorrow. Accountability keeps you and me from neglecting those "significant others" most important to us.

❏ *For Your Consideration:*

What are changes in family life that you're seeing to your own community? Your own church? Your own family?

What characteristics would you list to describe what you consider to be a strong and healthy family?

Family relationships are easily and commonly neglected. Why do you think neglecting family needs is so prevalent, even in many Christian homes?

What do the following verses tell us about family relationships:
Ephesians 5:22-6:4

Deuteronomy 6:4-9

1 Timothy 3:2-5, 11-12

Proverbs 22:6

God entrusts children to parents for their nurturing and preparation for a relationship with God. How might good parenting "pave the way" for a person's relationship with God? How might poor parenting hinder a person's ability to develop a relationship with God?

❏ *Time to Act:*

My goals for the way I relate to my family are:

9

Accountability In Five Dimensions: Personal

Wayne Schmidt

"Personal growth is creating an atmosphere in the various arenas of life that welcome the filling of the Holy Spirit in us. The spiritual life is not segregated from other dimensions of living, but is integral to them."

It's a law of life — if you're not growing, you're dying. It's a principle that our Creator has built into the masterpiece of nature. A sign of vitality is that which is dying away is being replaced and exceeded by that which is new.

As a child physically matures, we expect to see growth and change in his or her body. We would be alarmed if growth were stunted. Sometimes the growth process is gradual, and other times there are growth spurts. And there are growing pains!

For adults, growth is not as physical or dramatic. It is subtle but equally important. While physical growth can (and should!) diminish, other avenues of growth must be energized. We must continue to grow personally.

In the area of personal growth we will look at three arenas. All of these arenas are identified in Romans 12:1-2:

"Therefore, I urge you, brothers, in view of God's mercy, to offer your bodies as living sacrifices, holy and pleasing to God — this is your spiritual

act of worship. Do not conform any longer to the pattern of this world, but be transformed by the renewing of your mind. Then you will be able to test and approve what God's will is — his good, pleasing and perfect will" (NIV).

The first arena of personal life is the offering of our bodies. We are to care for ourselves physically and see our physical condition as a reflection of God's creation. Second, we are not to be conformed to this world, but to develop wholesome relationships which reinforce godly values and living. We should be growing socially as displayed in the depth and significance of our interaction with others. Third, we are to be renewing our minds. Our growth mentally in clear and biblical thinking is a key to personal renewal. These are the personal arenas of accountability — physical, social and mental.

Why isn't everyone growing personally? Simply put, growth involves change and change involves risk. It's easier at times to maintain the status quo than to move forward. Comfort zones are called that for a reason. Moving beyond them is uncomfortable. Change can be unsettling and threatening, yet it represents an exercise of faith. It is being confident that what God has begun to do in us He will finish.

Most people, when thinking of change, consider it to be something dramatic. This is called "disjunctive" change, or sudden change that is disruptive to life. However, most lasting changes are not revolutionary but evolutionary. They are the small, incremental adjustments that become deeply rooted in our perspective on and priorities in living.

Crash diets are one form of disjunctive change. They are extremely popular and their results show quickly. Lasting fitness, though, rarely comes through this approach. Pounds that melt away have a way of returning. Proper physical conditioning that remains is the product of slowly but surely changing one's eating and exercise habits. Dieting takes perseverance.

Personal growth is the by-product of persevering in practices that contribute to physical, social and mental development. Accountability reinforces our perseverance when our own willpower wanes.

❏ *Values Set The Vision!*

As Christians, we desire to be holy people. Holiness is directly related to wholeness, as the Apostle Paul clearly expounds:

"May God himself, the God of peace, sanctify you through and through.

May your whole spirit, soul and body be kept blameless at the coming of our Lord Jesus Christ" (1 Thessalonians 5:23 NIV).

Personal growth is creating an atmosphere in the various arenas of life that welcomes the fullness of the Holy Spirit in us. The spiritual life is not segregated from other dimensions of living, but is integral to them.

Our values set the vision and are rooted in God's will for us. We who know Christ care for ourselves physically and, not just because it is currently popular and is a "good idea." We acknowledge our bodies as the temple of the Holy Spirit and therefore seek to honor God with them (I Corinthians 6:19-20).

Let's face it — care for our physical bodies is the Achilles' heel of many Christians. We who would never abuse alcohol or drugs, abuse our bodies through gluttony. The addiction problem most pronounced in the Christian community is the inability to eat moderately and exercise properly. Our bulging waistlines prove harmful to us and our witness in the world. Carrying too much weight may even shorten our lives and limit our service to Him.

I do not encourage the "worship" of the human body. We live in a society that overvalues appearance and physical conditioning. This idolatry is evidenced in a preponderance of health clubs and an excessive devotion of time to physical development. I am saying that being devoted to Christ means maintaining a reasonable level of physical conditioning as an act of stewardship of the bodies He has created for us.

I express my vision this way: "I am physically fit, through proper diet, exercise and sleep, so that I might live as long and vitally as possible by God's plan." That is a statement of stewardship and my responsibility to God.

Socially, we develop relationships that will further Christ's work in us and others. God places us in significant relationships with others from the time we experience conversion. Simultaneously we become new creatures in Christ and new members of a spiritual family. We are part of the body of Christ with responsibilities to one another.

God works His transformation power in us in the context of close relationships which have a way of confronting us with who we really are. This confrontation happens in marriage. People are surprised to find out what their partner is really like in the day-to-day adventure of living together. They are even more surprised to find out what they themselves are really like! Marriage, the deepest of human relationships in God's creation, confronts us with the character issues of growth.

Aristotle claimed that friendship is "one soul in two bodies." One of the

deepest relationships in Scripture, that of Jonathan and David, came as the result of the knitting together of two kindred spirits. Real friendship takes commitment to share life. Many people who desire close relationships will never experience them due to an unwillingness to make necessary unselfish sacrifices.

Personal growth demands more than a breadth of acquaintances — it demands depth. Psychologist Rollo May estimates we meet five hundred to two thousand new acquaintances a year, but most people have fewer than seven personal friends. We need to move beyond superficiality to the place where we venture the risks of intimacy and vulnerability. How many people see the "real me"? How many do I give the right to confront me lovingly? The key is not in the number of friends I have but in building relationships with the right people who inspire me to live authentically.

Friendships change from time to time. Friendships breathe -sometimes we feel close and sometimes we feel distant. Not all relationships are lasting. But caution must be exercised lest we drift away from relationships for the wrong reasons, building and then discarding them purely on the basis of convenience or personal gain.

Let me again illustrate with the marriage relationship. One of the growing tendencies in our society is toward what has been labeled "serial monogamy." Spouses are selected to meet personal needs at various life stages — young adulthood, the middle-aged years and the retirement era. When life stages change, the spouse may change. A person is monogamous but may seek a series of marriages and divorces to meet his or her needs.

As Bible-believing Christians, we abhor that approach to marriage, but do we practice such when it comes to friendships? The temptation is to select friends who meet our needs in various life stages and situations, then cast them aside as our needs change. In the process, we forfeit the value of long-term commitment for the fleeting pleasure of selfish convenience.

When it comes to friendship, my statement of vision is to be "socially building deep and lasting friendships that make a difference both in this life and for eternity." I am not naturally a social butterfly — I tend to live a task-oriented, performance based life. I am growing to value and practice the truth that God has created us as social beings for our fulfillment and growth. Just as God's will is for us to be physically fit and socially active, it is His will for us to be mentally alert and active. Philippians 4:8 tells us:

"Finally, brothers, whatever is true, whatever is noble, whatever is right, whatever is pure, whatever is lovely, whatever is admirable — if anything is excellent or praiseworthy — think about such things" (NIV).

Think about such things. The word think in this instance means to "meditate on, give continuous attention to, be occupied with, mull over." It

means much more than a passing thought! One of the greatest reasons for discontentment is spiritual empty-headedness, leaving the mind as unoccupied territory and an easy target for counterproductive or sinful thoughts. We are to "take captive every thought to make it obedient to Christ" (2 Corinthians 10:5 NIV).

Growing mentally involves obtaining knowledge, but there is so much more! It is managing our attitudes which are so determinative in our desire to reflect Christ to others. I must confess that for years I've considered positive thinkers to be intellectual "flakes" and "featherweights." But I've come to discover that a truly positive attitude is not the function of a denial of reality, but a commitment to experience that reality in light of the resources available in Christ.

Michigan is America's "winter wonderland," and I greatly enjoy the variety of seasons. About February, however, as the snow and consecutive number of gloomy days increase, people's attitudes tend to turn negative. They have even given a name to this phenomenon - Seasonal Affective Disorder (SAD). The lack of light and activity create a depressing effect. People are influenced by their environment. A point of growth for all of us, however, is when the environmental effects on our attitude are secondary to the influence of God's Spirit on our minds and moods. God's Spirit provides the basis of positive thinking!

The mind is not disconnected from the spirit. Many a closed mind can be directly traced to an unteachable spirit. An unteachable spirit is not a "mental problem" but the evidence of an inward arrogance and carnal pride that imagines one's superiority to others. Only genuine repentance can remedy this sinful malady and clear the way for renewing of the mind.

My statement of vision is "to be mentally stretching in order to think broader and clearer." Mental growth involves a need for accountability in accumulating knowledge and managing attitudes. When I combine mental acuity with caring for myself physically and developing socially, I become a growing person!

❏ *Goals Guide Growth!*

Our vision shapes our values, but our goals move us from philosophical investigation to practical implementation. Let's begin with the physical arena of personal growth, because most of us are experienced in this area. Most of us have set goals for dieting and exercise more times than we care or dare to remember!

❑ ❑ ❑ ❑ ❑ ❑ ❑ ❑

❑ *Richard Simmons or Arnold Schwarzenegger?*

What do we seek to accomplish with our goals for physical conditioning? Is our target to be thin and "wimpy" like Richard Simmons or well-muscled and "macho" like Arnold Schwarzenegger? While some folk may desire to hone athletic skills or build muscular bodies in order to impress others, most of us seek a reasonable level of fitness that enables us to "live all the life" God has granted to us.

Good fitness is a combination of proper diet, exercise, and rest. It takes perseverance and accountability. Few of us left to ourselves naturally "drift" toward these painful disciplines. Characteristics like moderation and balance require energy, attention, and great sacrifice.

A proper diet is a matter of what we eat, how we eat, and when we eat. We are bombarded with information on cholesterol, fat, and calories which can prove helpful in selecting the foods we need to eat. It isn't an act of faith to sit down to a meal of greasy foods to be washed down with a high-sugared drink and finished off with a high-cholesterol dessert — and then pray for God to bless it — it's an act of foolishness!

Often the simplest of practices in dieting can make a big difference over time. One might be to carefully fill your plate, and then eat only what is on your plate with no second helpings. Another might be not to eat anything after supper. Desserts could be limited to twice a week.

For maximum effect, dieting must be combined with exercise. To be beneficial, exercise must be regular and occur a minimum of three times a week. Choosing something you enjoy makes follow through more likely. A family physician can advise you regarding the most appropriate exercise to stimulate your circulatory system and tone your muscles without jeopardizing your health.

Diet and exercise help us to get within and to maintain a proper weight range. For my age and frame, a proper range is from 152-155 pounds. When I get under 152, I'm free to eat a little more. When I exceed 155, I need to escalate my exercise and cut back on my eating. I like the flexibility of a weight range because it accommodates the "ebb and flow" of my eating habits. I know when holidays are approaching I'd better get to the low end of my range because by the time they're done I'll be at the high end!

In my accountability partnership, I regularly share my weight and the frequency of my exercise since we've last met. I've added to that accountability by working out with someone else, usually a co-worker, and letting him see the scales at weigh-in time. There are many times I've gone to the fitness center because someone would be waiting for me!

Combined with proper diet and exercise is the need for rest. Resting well involves many factors including regularity in our sleeping schedule, effective stress management, and being spiritually right with the Lord (Proverbs 3:1-12). While I try to get by on as little sleep as possible and still maintain personal health, I still require more sleep than most men my age. Every once in a while, I try to lower my amount of sleep for fifteen minutes a night for a couple of weeks. If I feel fine mentally, emotionally, and physically, I've added fifteen minutes to my day!

It can be dangerous to sleep too little. Some people who sleep too little, yet get by physically fail to recognize how the lack of sleep impacts their moods, thoughts, and relationships. Research has shown that a long-term experience of too little sleep can undermine our creativity and sensitivity. Good, balanced stewardship demands that we get all the sleep we need, but only what we need.

What are some possible accountability goals in physical fitness? Here are some suggestions that may help you create your own objectives:

❑ I will submit to a complete medical examination by _____.
❑ I will maintain a weight range of _____ pounds.
❑ I will exercise for at least _____ minutes _____ nonconsecutive days each week.
❑ I will limit my daily calorie intake to _____.
❑ I will schedule a regular appointment with the dentist by_____.
❑ I will have a bedtime snack only _____ day(s) a week.
❑ I will cease _____ (unhealthy habit — smoking, dependence on caffeine, non-prescription drugs) by _____.
❑ I will walk (or jog or bike) _____ miles a week.
❑ I will sleep _____ hours for _____ nights a week, generally between the hours of ____ p.m. and ____ a.m.

There are endless possibilities! Physical goals should identify proper weight, diet, exercise, and sleep — then become accountable for them!

❑ *Foster Fulfilling Friendships*

Because we have superficial contact with so many people, most of us will have to target certain people with whom we will intentionally spend time and energy to develop relationships. We should not substitute a great quantity of acquaintances for the priority of having a few good "quality" friends.

Some of us who have difficulty developing friendships may need to identify some means of interacting with people. If we are one dimensional people, absorbed in our careers or personal interests, building genuine friendships may be difficult. I've recently developed the commitment to play some golf and tennis, and not because I had too much spare time on my hands. I have found that these activities tend to provide comfortable, enjoyable channels through which I can cultivate acquaintances and form friendships.

I meet many people in my pastoral ministry. My desire is to be more personable in my professional associations with individuals. That's one reason I'm a participant in a small group each week and not the leader. I desire to be not only a pastor, but a friend. That means being honest, open, and transparent — creating communication that is a dynamic two-way street.

For Christians, relationships have not only social but spiritual significance. I've discovered praying regularly for friends develops a spiritual bond that keeps me sensitive to their needs from the Lord's perspective. Building relationships with unbelievers can provide opportunities for sharing Christ, moving beyond being spiritual "hit-men" to displaying the fruit of the Spirit in the context of a sincere friendship.

While friendships may "come naturally," they can be enhanced by intentional commitment. Possible goals include:

- ❑ To spend at least one hour alone with _____ each month.
- ❑ To involve myself in _____ (hobby, sport, etc.) on a _____ (monthly, weekly) basis for the purpose of facilitating relationships.
- ❑ To invite to our home one other family from our church each month.
- ❑ To pray for _____ as my friend(s) on an average of _____ weekly

In formulating goals, identify friends or people who might become friends, and commit yourself to the actions that would best help that friendship develop.

❏ *Mental Midget Or Mental Giant?*

Much of our mental capability is genetically predetermined. Most of us will never be geniuses or candidates for the Mensa Society, which requires an I.Q. of 160 or above. However, our goals should help us develop the mental potential God has given each one of us.

One possible option is to set a realistic goal for reading books. That goal could be one a month or any number representing an attainable, yet challenging, goal. My personal goal is to read twenty-five books a year and keep a "log" of my reading. The log helps me to both recall what I've read and to see if I'm falling into a reading "rut."

While we may choose to read mostly one type of book (self-help, business, religious, etc.), we can help ourselves by intermixing some subjects to expand our horizons. One way we as a church staff hold each other accountable for reading is to pick out a book and spend one-half hour a week discussing a particular chapter. We've read books on leadership and management, counseling, prayer, and ministry to name but a few. Not all of these books are written from a Christian perspective, and that diversity helps keep us in touch with our world.

I enjoy reading books on leadership and ministry the most, but choosing only those topics would limit my view of the world. I am not a connoisseur of science and history. My in-laws give me a subscription to the "Smithsonian" magazine each year to broaden my reading horizons.

Where do we find time to read the newspaper as well as books? For many, that time is available only at the "flip of a switch" — the "off" switch on the television! Limiting our TV time or devoting our attention to more educational programming would prove a major step forward for many of us!

Seminars and educational programs represent another way to achieve mental stimulation. Many communities offer "lifetime learning" courses. Continuing education is a requirement in many professions, so institutions of higher learning are offering more flexible schedules to accommodate the adult learner. Career transitions are more common and often education is the doorway to the greatest opportunities.

I've witnessed the changes taking place in my profession, especially in seminaries designing programs compatible with a full-time pastor's schedule and the proliferation of professional doctoral programs. It took me eight years to get my master's degree and will require seven years to obtain my doctorate — and it's not just because I'm a little slow! My goal is to be in a formal setting of continuing education until I'm forty years of age while remaining in the ministry. I've chosen seminaries which accommodate that goal.

One of the best ways to "stretch" mentally is to teach. Whether it's discipling a person one-on-one or standing in front of a class, communicating to others forces clarification of our thoughts. I'm finding that to be true in my own life right now. I've preached and practiced accountability for years, but writing this book designed to teach accountability concepts causes me to think harder and hopefully more clearly!

We need to keep a teachable spirit and avoid the "expert" syndrome. People who consider themselves experts often know the least. I was an expert on parenting — until I had children. I was an expert on pastoring — until I was called to lead a church. One of my favorite definitions of an "expert" is anyone carrying a briefcase more than fifty miles from home! We are not "experts," but people growing in a lifelong adventure of learning. Here are options for goals to keep you stretching mentally:

❏ I will read _____ books a _____.
❏ I will seek to read at least one book from the following areas:
_____ (possibilities include religion, self-help, psychology, history, business, current events, etc.)
❏ I will limit my television viewing to _____ hours a week.
❏ I will enroll in a class on _____ by _____.
❏ I will include at least one educational program in my television viewing each week.
❏ I will attend a day-long seminar on _____ by _____.
❏ I will utilize our community library for books or cassettes at least once a month.
❏ I will seek a mentor in the area of _____ and meet with him or her at least _____ times this year.

Design goals that will develop you professionally, personally, and spiritually.

❏ *Keep Growing!*

Growing people inspire those around them to grow, positively affecting the family, business, church or neighborhood of which they are a part. Stagnant people have at best a neutral effect, and most often a negative effect. Like stagnant ponds, it is easier for decay to take place than growth.

People who refuse to grow often feel threatened by growing people. They feel they are being surpassed and experience the temptation to hold their friend back. Isn't it amazing the number of relationships that survive when one person fails, but fall apart when one person succeeds? The envy and jealousy precipitated by a friend's growth threaten the very foundation of friendship. We are to rejoice with those who rejoice and mourn with those who mourn (Romans 12:15). How unfortunate that the mourning comes easier than the rejoicing — revealing secret struggles with discontentment, covetousness, and poor self-esteem.

We must be growing people. Sometimes that may mean we'll "grow together" with a person; sometimes we'll "grow apart." We all need to grow up — physically, mentally and socially — into people who honor Christ with our lives.

What about you? Can you target some areas where you need to grow up? Accountability will help you take those "initially painful, ultimately rewarding" steps of growth. Be courageous and move forward into areas God has probably already shown you are needed for continued personal development.

❏ *For Your Consideration:*

Many people express a desire to be a growing person. How would you describe someone you consider to be a growing person? Why isn't everyone growing personally?

What are some of the costs of being a growing person? What are the costs of not growing as a person?

❏ ❏ ❏ ❏ ❏ ❏ ❏ ❏

There's a saying that "some people eat to live and some people live to eat." How would a person know if food has become too important or addictive?

What are barriers to meaningful and lasting relationships? Why do so many Christians have so few non-Christian friends, and how might this hinder the spread of the gospel?

Growing mentally involves cultivating a teachable spirit. What attitudes and actions might help a person remain teachable?

❏ *Time to act:*

My goal(s) for the well-being of my physical body:

My goal(s) for developing meaningful relationships:

My goal(s) for stretching mentally:

Accountability In Five Dimensions:
Professional/Financial

Wayne Schmidt

"God's Word reveals a direct connection between our financial and professional actions and our commitment to Jesus Christ."

It was an eye-opening experience! During the first few years of my ministry, I had lunch one day with a businessman in our community. He is a committed Christian who seeks to honor the Lord by the way he manages his company. He shared with me one of his greatest disappointments — the times he had been "left holding the bag" by pastors who failed to follow through on their financial commitments.

I could sense his emotion as he attempted to reconcile in his mind how those "spiritual leaders" could be so financially irresponsible. I had a hollow feeling and silently hoped that his experience was the exception, not the rule.

That early experience helped forge a commitment in my life. Financial management is vitally linked to personal and spiritual integrity. I will not compromise my witness or ministry by failing to be a good steward financially.

I also discovered another common perception of ministers — "they work only on Sundays!" While often spoken in jest or the result of misperception of what the ministry involves, some people have witnessed a woefully

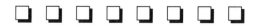

deficient "work ethic" in their pastors. There is so little direct accountability for how a pastor spends his time that the temptation to "slack off" is ever present.

I share these experiences with no intent of downgrading ministers or the ministerial profession. I thank God consistently that He has called me to serve Him in this way. I feel guilty at times for taking a paycheck for something I enjoy so much — but I always take it!

These experiences point out that it is impossible to live a life of integrity and authenticity without accountability in the professional and financial arenas of life. It has been suggested that the best way to determine a person's true character and commitment is not by reading his or her prayer journal, but by examining personal financial records. How would you or I look if our work record or our checkbooks were public knowledge? Would such revelations enhance our testimony to Christ?

No wonder the Bible talks so much about money. John MacArthur, pastor of Grace Community Church in Pomona City, California, reveals these biblical statistics in his tape series "Mastery of Materialism":

"Sixteen out of thirty-eight of Christ's parables relate to money, more is said in the New Testament about money than about heaven and hell combined; five times more is said about money than prayer, there are over two thousand verses dealing with money and possessions."

God's Word reveals a direct connection between our financial or professional actions and our commitment to Jesus Christ.

We need to establish clear values and goals related to our jobs and money. We live in a changing world, and those changes will only accelerate, especially when it comes to careers. We can expect to see:

❏ More women in the workplace, as they increasingly attain the highest positions of leadership in the corporate world.

❏ With the advent of computers with modems, FAX machines, and other technological advances, there will be more home-based work than ever, avoiding long commuting times and expensive central offices. Not only will work be more home-based, but even car-based with cellular phones and portable computers!

❏ Career changes will be more frequent, averaging four to six times for the average adult. Many are now exiting college with the expectation of changing jobs about once every decade.

❏ There will be more "flex-time" schedules, with the employee able to negotiate when work days begin and end, and how long they last.

In a changing world, clear values and goals help us steer the course most pleasing to God.

This chapter focuses on both the professional and financial dimensions of life. The two are inseparable. A major motivation in job selection for Americans continues to be the "financial package," with reliable surveys indicating an increasing number of college students seeking careers which will enable them to be well-off financially. But money is not the only motivation in working — personal development and a sense of fulfillment are also "high priority." For the Christian, honoring Christ with our work and finances is to be the highest priority (1 Corinthians 10:31, Colossians 3:17).

❏ *Values Set The Vision*

I'm grateful that increasing attention is being given to applying God's Word to financial and professional decisions. Authors like Ron Blue and Larry Burkett are helping equip the body of Christ to be better stewards. There is a hunger to honor God in these areas. Our church's largest adult Sunday School class recently spent three months looking at career and money concerns from a biblical perspective. We must clarify our values, identify our goals, and then be accountable to act in accordance with our plans.

❏ *Make Your Boss Look Good!*

People work from a variety of motives. The most selfish and maybe the most common is to "make me look good." The attention is given to the high-visibility items that will put a person in good standing for a promotion, pay raise, or positive career transition. Secret compromises are viewed as necessary when they help to lift the compromiser to the next "rung" on the "corporate ladder." "Everybody does it, I've got to fit in" is a common rationalization for cutting corners in matters of integrity.

A higher motive is to work to make your supervisor or company "look good." This certainly has the overtones of a servant's spirit and may result in denying yourself personal credit in order to transfer acclaim to another.

The highest motive is to work and live to make the boss "look good." For whom does the Christian really work? Who is the ultimate boss? The Scriptures mince no words.

"Whatever you do, work at it with all your heart, as working for the Lord, not for men, since you know that you will receive an inheritance from the Lord as a reward. It is the Lord Christ you are serving (Colossians 3:23-24).

We are to work in a way that inspires people to thank God and glorify Him. That's a lofty value — and a lifelong challenge!

In our work ethic, there are two extremes to avoid. One extreme is laziness. The book of Proverbs unflatteringly labels the lazy person a "sluggard." For such folk, more energy is given to avoiding work and making excuses (Proverbs 22:13) than to earning a paycheck!

This temptation is especially enticing for persons who do not have enough work to fill their days or whose compensation is far below their performance. I live in a state famous for large automobile factories. While many conscientious workers fill these plants, stories surface of workers having production quotas filled before shifts are half completed. Workers then sleep, read, or play games. It's tough to work with intensity and integrity when the challenge is just not there!

We live among people who not only expect "nice" possessions, but feel they deserve them — often whether they've worked for them or not. Parents do their children no favor when they cater to their every whim without expecting them to work. "The sluggard craves and gets nothing, but the desires of the diligent are fully satisfied" (Proverbs 13:4).

If one extreme is laziness, the other is "workaholism." This is the "all work and no play" syndrome. Worldly success is often pictured as wealth coming from superhuman commitment to work, no matter how much personal health, family wholeness, and spiritual vibrancy are neglected in the process.

Having benefitted from a strong Christian background, I avoided many of the addictions that plague our society — except this one. I am a "recovering workaholic." Somewhere I picked up the idea that my personal value is based on my performance, and like so many others battling this extreme, I had a performance-based self-esteem for years. I could camouflage it because, after all, I was doing "God's work!"

Workaholism is an addiction. It is relying on something outside of one's self and God in order to cope with life. Overwork can leave us especially vulnerable to other temptations with the subtle impression "I've worked hard — so I deserve it!"

Through my accountability relationship, God has brought more balance to my life. To a workaholic, "non-work activities" seem unnatural. I've

needed to structure time for friends, family, recreation and renewal. My attitudes are now being shaped by acting on my priorities, and a balanced life is becoming much more satisfying than a life absorbed in career pursuits.

A healthy, balanced professional life is important to us and to God. God uses our career to develop our character. Through wrestling with its temptations and interacting with people, we are refined and edified. God also uses our career to develop contacts — people whom we may influence toward a relationship with Christ by our work and words. For most Christians, their greatest interaction with unbelievers is at their place of employment. What an opportunity to demonstrate the reality of the difference Jesus Christ can make!

I have carefully worded the values that I pray will characterize my professional life:

❏ I desire to have a growing impact in the lives of others, influencing them not only for today but for eternity.
❏ I will work with a high degree of integrity and accountability, avoiding the pitfall of hypocrisy.
❏ I will minister with creativity and excellence, setting aside personal "comfort zones" to extend God's Kingdom.
❏ I seek to be humble, giving God the glory for whatever results may come from being obedient to His calling and anointing upon my life.

I ask God daily to help me to work with these motives instead of working only for personal gain, competition, or in response to the urgent. What values would you identify to guide your professional life?

❏ *Watch Those French Fries!*

A U.S. Congressman took his son out to a fast-food restaurant and bought him lunch. When they were seated at the table, this congressman reached over to take one of the french fries he had purchased for his son. His son got perturbed with his dad for taking his french fries.

As the congressman later reflected on that incident, he came to the conclusion that his young son failed to recognize three truths:
1. He doesn't realize I can get all the french fries I want without him.
2. He doesn't realize I have the power to take not one, but all of his fries

111

away from him.

3. He doesn't understand the source of those french fries — he thinks I'm a thief!

When John Maxwell shared this illustration in his "Successful Stewardship" seminar, I knew the application, and so do you. All we need to do is put God in place of the Congressman, and possessions in the place of french fries. We then have a revealing picture of many people's perspective on money — maybe even our perspective! The foundational values in guiding our use of money should be God's ownership and our stewardship. God is the owner of all that we have. All that we earn comes from resources He has provided. Even our ability to breathe, think, and move are the result of His grace and generosity to us.

Because He is the owner, we have the responsibility to be good stewards — careful managers of the portion of all God's wealth that He has entrusted directly to us. Failure either to manage His resources wisely or to return a portion to Him through giving is robbery (Malachi 3:8-10).

Now when I picture robbery, I think of armed robbery or shoplifting! I don't think that's the image of robbing God that's most helpful. Robbing God is more like stealing through embezzlement — "to appropriate (as property entrusted to one's care) fraudulently to one's own use." We take resources God has entrusted to us for His purposes and use them for our purposes. We use what belongs to Him to build our kingdom rather than His Kingdom.

Few people intentionally start out to rob God. It's just so easy to get carried away in that ever present desire for more. "On the average, American households feel they need $8,000 - $11,000 more income annually to live comfortably." I personally have felt that tug. I have served the church which I pastor from its beginning. In the initial days, my salary was modest. As the church has grown, the lay leaders have made sure that my compensation has also increased. I believe I am well compensated for my responsibilities, and yet still carry that myth in my mind that I "need just a little more."

Ron Blue is on target when he shares that money is a tool, a test, and a testimony. As a tool, it is not an end in itself, but a means to a higher end. It is a test of our trust in God and our ability to manage what belongs to Him. We're reminded of the "trust test" every time we glance at a coin imprinted with "In God We Trust."

Money is also a testimony of the identity of our true Master and Lord. Jesus said it best:

"No one can serve two masters. Either he will hate the one and love the other, or he will be devoted to one and despise the other. You cannot serve both God and money" (Matthew 6:24).

No wonder Jesus said "For where your treasure is, there will your heart be also" (Matthew 6:21).

Managing what belongs to God is more than a matter of giving. God, in His generosity, desires that what belongs to Him also be a blessing to us. After we have honored Him first through our giving, He welcomes us to utilize His resources for the good of ourselves and our families.

For years the 10/10/80 principle has been set forth as a guideline. It can be summarized as follows:

10% is returned to the Lord first as a tithe, a concrete way of demonstrating that all I have belongs to Him.

10% is saved to provide funds for future goals such as travel, retirement, education, and home ownership.

80% is to be used to support current lifestyle demands. Now these percentages are not "written in stone." They may vary based on incomes and stage of life. For instance, a young person anticipating purchasing a home may save more than 10%, while an older person saving 10% may border on hoarding. There are stages of life for accumulating resources and stages for preserving or distributing resources. I know many people who give away much more than 10% of their income. I also know people who unfortunately allow their current lifestyle to consume over 100% of their income, financing the rest through credit.

So we need to state our values clearly when it comes to our material resources. I've identified the following for myself this year:

❏ I will recognize God's ownership of everything through careful stewardship (management) of what He has directly entrusted to me.

❏ I seek to increase my percentage of giving by decreasing the percentage spent to maintain current lifestyle demands.

❏ I will design my budget so that it nourishes the priorities in other areas of my life.

Let me clarify my last "value statement." If I value my family, what percentage of my budget goes to build family health and create family memories? If I want to further my family's education, have I made provision for it? If I value my health, do I have funding to belong to the YMCA or purchase exercise equipment? Without financial resources, lofty values become hollow statements. How might you express your financial values?

❏ *Goals Guide Growth*

In looking at the professional and financial dimensions, we've discussed values that shape our attitudes. Because it is impossible to be accountable to another just for values, we need specific goals that can guide us in each of these arenas of life.

❏ *Needed: Professional Goals*

While many accountability goals will be quite consistent from year to year, goals in the professional area often require greater flexibility. Goal-setting here depends, of course, on how often one changes jobs or how often a person's "job description" changes. I like to choose each year what I would identify as a "focal point" of professional growth. That will be the subject of my professional accountability that year, and then, depending on my success, I choose another area for the coming year.

One year that focal point was "conflict management." I became aware that I was uncomfortable when people strongly expressed differing viewpoints. I tended to suppress conflict and often ended up keeping my mouth shut inappropriately. So that year I took a course "Power, Change, and Conflict Management." I sought others' evaluations of how I tended to interact in discussions involving different viewpoints. I led our church board in a study of managing conflict and change with the church.

Another year I focused on becoming more relational in my ministry. As a result, I disciplined myself to delegate more of my administrative work. I built a list of people with whom I wanted to meet. I initiated more social contacts.

Sometimes the focal point I choose is designed to capitalize on a strength already present in my life. Other times it is an attempt to neutralize the impact of a weakness in my ministry. I choose the area, but often ask others for input regarding the appropriateness of the area I've selected.

What are some goals that might apply to your job? Here are suggestions to stimulate your thinking:

> ❏ I will get to work fifteen minutes before starting time in order to better prepare for a productive day.

❏ ❏ ❏ ❏ ❏ ❏ ❏ ❏

- ❏ I will give my employer an honest day's work, limiting "free" or "personal" time (chatting with others, nonbusiness phone calls, etc) to _____ minutes a day.
- ❏ I will speak a word of encouragement to _____ once each work day.
- ❏ I will be honest when filling out my expense accounts.
- ❏ I will not complain about my work unless it is in the form of a suggestion to someone who has the power to effect change.
- ❏ I will take a class or seminar on _____ this year to improve my job skills.
- ❏ Once a month I will write a note of appreciation to someone with whom or for whom I work.

Adapt these to apply to your career situation or personal professional needs.

I am accountable to my partner for certain areas of professional growth. But I also initiate accountability with those who supervise me. In my case, that's our local church board of administration. Twice a year I meet with each board member individually to have him or her evaluate my personal life and professional work. This openness has led to a very good and positive relationship with the board during the years I've served as pastor. And it has led to many great insights for me which I seek to implement in my personal and professional growth.

❏ *Needed: Financial Goals*

I perform many wedding ceremonies in the course of a year. I enjoy meeting with young couples in premarital counseling sessions and sensing their enthusiasm and anticipation for the days ahead. I have the responsibility of tempering that wonderful idealism with a touch of realism. That includes helping them be realistic about money.

I've married couples who were debt-free, only to have them return a year or so later with hundreds (or thousands) of dollars in unmanageable debt. That places a tremendous strain on a new, growing relationship. The "debt trap" is one reason I'm so motivated to push couples to craft a written budget even before they are married.

Written budgets force folk to be realistic. They push us to clarify our priorities. They foster communication about our expectations. I've

encouraged couples to write down what they believe is a reasonable amount to spend annually in various areas. One couple, in the budget category of clothing, discovered how different their values were. He wrote down $200 annually and she wrote down $2000 annually. That's an $1800 difference — and potential source of irritation and conflict!

Do you have a written budget? Check with your Christian bookstore for resources by such persons as Ron Blue or Larry Burkett to guide you. A written budget is not a means of bondage, but a road map to freedom. Your goals and budget could be divided into the three areas we discussed earlier — giving, saving, and living expenses.

I'm often asked where a person should direct his or her giving. Most of us receive far more requests for money than we could ever hope to honor. The Old Testament people did not have radio, television, direct mail, and support letters. They brought their money to the storehouse, the temple — and there was only one temple!

There is still a temple to which we are to bring our tithe. 1 Peter 2:5 tells us:

"You also, like living stones, are being built into a spiritual house to be a holy priesthood, offering spiritual sacrifices acceptable to God through Jesus Christ."

That temple (spiritual house) is the gathering together of believers in whom Christ lives. Believers gather together in local churches and there build up each other. The first ten percent of my income goes to my local church. It is then the collective body of believers who decide in the annual church budget planning how those resources can best be used. I give up personal control over the use of that tithe in order to work with others in discerning God's will.

There is another temple identified in the New Testament. 1 Corinthians 6:19-20a tells us:

"Do you not know that your body is the temple of the Holy Spirit, who is in you, whom you have received from God? You are not your own; you were bought at a price."

Each of us personally is a temple of God, a truth which should impact the way we live and the way we give.

Beyond my tithe to the local church, I believe God has called me to support certain causes and people. Notice I said "beyond my tithe." If I just redistribute the first ten percent I give, that denies needed funds to my local church and does nothing to stretch me. I'm simply cutting the same pie a different way! I want God to burden my heart with certain causes and allow

me to make a sacrifice to fund them, not make my church sacrifice to do so. Such additional personal giving comes from the eighty percent allotted to support my lifestyle.

The second area is saving. It's hard to accept slow, measured progress in a "get rich quick" world. A book on getting rich slowly would certainly not be a bestseller! Yet that's the biblical way. Proverbs 13:1 tells us that "dishonest money dwindles away, but he who gathers money little by little makes it grow." The little piggy bank that hung above my grandparents' table bore these words: "A penny saved is a penny earned."

We save in a variety of ways and for a variety of causes.

Most of us need to save for worthy causes such as retirement, funding a college education, purchasing a home, or even paying cash for items like appliances and automobiles. We can save by putting money in the bank or utilizing other investment vehicles. Or we can save by the early payoff of high-interest consumer debt or prepaying on our home mortgage.

The third area in which we need specific goals in our budget relates to our living expenses. It may take two or three years to develop this budget area accurately and fully. It requires great discipline to put a "ceiling" on our standard of living and postpone desired purchases — discipline that needs reinforcement through accountability.

My accountability partner reviews my total written budget each year and is free to question any area. He looks over my giving, my saving, and my living expenses. (It helps that he is a Certified Financial Planner!) It is also evidence of the trust I place in him after many years of accountability. Most of all, such accountability provides reinforcement when my willpower begins to waver.

What are possible financial goals? Here are a few to consider:

- ❏ I will give $_____ to my local church in the coming year.
- ❏ I will give $_____ to _____ (person or cause) each month.
- ❏ I will save $_____ from each paycheck and place it in a savings account.
- ❏ I will keep a spending diary of items costing over $1 in order to more accurately assess where my money is spent.
- ❏ I will pay an extra $_____ on the principal balance of my home mortgage each month.
- ❏ I will eliminate all credit card debt by _____ (date)
- ❏ I will purchase _____ with cash by saving $_____ from

each paycheck.

The goals you formulate should correspond to your current financial situation, desired purchases, family needs, and stage in life. Be sure they are not only a path to your dreams but represent what you believe is God's will for you.

❏ *The Bottom Line*

Edwin Land, the founder of Polaroid, stood before a shareholder's meeting in 1977. After they had heard desperate reports regarding a product reversal, he calmly and convincingly responded by saying "The bottom line is in heaven."

What a truth to remember in our professional pursuits and financial decisions!

"To the man who pleases Him, God gives wisdom, knowledge and happiness, but to the sinner He gives the task of gathering and storing up wealth to hand it over to the one who pleases God" (Ecclesiastes 2:26).

So, how about getting started? What is the next step for you? Balancing a checkbook? Developing a budget? Making a list of strengths and weaknesses in your professional life?

These actions can be hard to initiate — they may war against our natural inclinations. Accountability will help you get started — and keep growing. The rewards will be not only financial, but eternal!

❏ *For Your Consideration:*

How might a person "working for the Lord" (Colossians 3:23-24) work and act differently than a person just working for the money?

What is the difference between working hard and being a "workaholic?"

❏ ❏ ❏ ❏ ❏ ❏ ❏ ❏

Malachi 3:8-10 teaches us:
Matthew 6:21 teaches us:
Matthew 6:24 teaches us:

The Bible teaches the wisdom of giving and saving — today's world emphasizes borrowing. What are the long-term consequences of God's way vs. the world's way? How does managing money God's way help develop discipline, character and proper priorities?

How can a written budget benefit an individual and/or family?

❏ *Time to act:*

My goal(s) for the way I manage my money:

My goal(s) for professional development:

11
CREATING A PARTNERSHIP

Wayne Schmidt

"It is the people that make an accountability relationship effective. There is no program or process that will substitute for people of character."

People are hungry for relationships. Tired of superficial acquaintances, they are expressing a desire to fellowship with people in a way that really makes a difference. They talk regularly about being too busy and how they long for more time to really share with people.

For many, it's all talk. The trend of our society is toward people who long for significant life-changing relationships, and yet are less willing than ever to make the necessary commitments of time and energy. They want the return on relationships without the investment.

We see a gap between desire and commitment at our church. People attend out of appreciation for the atmosphere of acceptance and verbalize a need for deeper Christian relationships. Because our church is quite large, we make it clear that you cannot build relationships if you just attend a morning worship service. It's necessary to attend (1) a CONNECTION (age-graded adult classes which meet during the Sunday School hour), (2) a small group, or (3) fellowship events in order to form friendships. Months later, I'll discover they're leaving our church — because "we just weren't friendly." I

also discover they've never invested time and energy beyond attending a morning worship service.

Creating an accountability partnership can be one of the most rewarding experiences in life. But it requires a commitment, an investment of one's time and energy. No partnership is stronger than the commitment of the weakest partner.

While this chapter will focus in on the one-to-one partnerships, I've seen accountability work well in groups of up to five people. Most of the practices and principles of this chapter apply to small accountability groups as well as partnerships.

The strength of an accountability relationship is in finding a good partner and in being a good partner. Be sure you're ready to measure up to those qualities you look for in others. Remember the Golden Rule "Do unto others as you would have them do unto you."

❏ *What is an Accountability Partner?*

One of the keys to finding what you're looking for is knowing what you're looking for! Whatever your mind envisions for a partnership will form your expectations for that relationship. Any relationship with a serious mismatch of expectations is in for some challenging, if not frustrating, days!

Perhaps the best place to start is in identifying what an accountability partnership is not. First of all, an accountability partner is not necessarily a mentor. A tendency for many is to want to form this covenant with a "spiritual giant" they admire. Mentors are quite valuable as examples to us and can provide accountability. I have had several mentors over the years who have helped me to develop specific areas of my life and ministry. Accountability, however, seems to work best in a peer relationship. There should be a rough "equality" in spiritual development and overall maturity. The peer relationship contributes to the accountability being mutual, which is important in a lasting relationship.

Neither is an accountability partner necessarily a close friend. Friends are probably the people we think of most readily and naturally when considering a partner. Be careful. Sometimes a close friendship hinders a person's ability to be objective or confront lovingly. Some of our best friends are much too forgiving, which may be what makes them our best friends!

When Paul and I first formed our partnership, we were acquaintances but not close friends. We respected one another but had not spent much

122

time together socially. Our friendship has grown over the years as a by-product of our accountability, which is an added blessing. Often a close friendship will develop from a partnership but it is not required, and perhaps not even recommended, in initiating an accountability relationship.

An accountability partner is what the name indicates — a partner. That person serves to reinforce your will power in living according to your established priorities and goals. It is someone you respect and whom you would not want to disappoint. It is a person who makes you feel guilty if you don't follow through on your commitments — feel guilty, that is, in a motivating sort of way!

❏ *What Makes A Match?*

Careful selection is the foundation of a lasting partnership. Finding the right partner takes patience and prayer. An impulsive choice may well lead to the discomfort of having to discontinue a relationship prematurely.

A wise man once gave me this advice for selecting employees for our church — "The best time to fire them is before you hire them." It was his way of encouraging me to invest time and energy before the commitment was made in order to avoid the frustration of hiring a person who doesn't work out. While selecting a partner is not an employment process, it requires the same kind of diligence in determining a "good fit."

There are four factors that people should keep in mind when searching for a partner. The first is AVAILABILITY. Schedules are more hectic and varied than ever before. Some people work days, some people work nights. Many start their work week by hopping on a plane and don't return home until Friday afternoon. Others work "swing shifts" and have difficulty predicting their work schedules.

Will your schedules match to the point that you can meet on a regular basis? And are the times that work out really opportune times? Breakfast meetings are good if you're both "morning persons", or evenings are fine if neither of you fade away mentally when the sun goes down. Make sure that there are workable times when each is not only available but reasonably alert.

A second could be called the AFFINITY factor. This relates to having certain characteristics in common. A primary affinity factor for accountability relationships is that people should be of the same gender. There are many personal and spiritual dangers in forming an accountability

partnership with a member of the opposite sex. It would (and should) limit the depth of discussion that could take place.

It is often helpful to be in the same life stage or have children who are approximately the same age. Parents of preschoolers face different challenges than parents of teenagers. Life while you're "thirtysomething" is different from life while you're "fiftysomething." The basis of sharing is broader with affinity in age.

There are many other affinity factors — career interests, hobbies, recreational activities, economic situations — that should be taken into consideration. You're not looking for a "clone" but you are seeking some common denominators in life.

This affinity is also vital in a small group. In addition to my accountability partnership, I meet with four other men in a group called "Iron Men" (Proverbs 27:17 — "As iron sharpens iron, so one man sharpens another.") on a regular basis. All of them are businessmen with an entrepreneurial flair. They all place importance on being physically fit, are married, and within a few years of the same age. They all share the ultimate affinity factor — a commitment to Jesus Christ as Lord of life.

A third factor when investigating a match is INTENSITY. Some of us are hard chargers and some of us like to relax. Some cut right to the bottom line and others enjoy small talk. As the old joke puts it — "Some make things happen, some let things happen and some ask 'what happened?'" How intense are you about accountability and how intense do you want your partner to be?

We've noticed this difference in small groups in our church.

Our Navigators 2:7 discipleship groups have a high level of accountability requiring Scripture memorization and certain spiritual activity. Our Pastoral Care groups are more relaxed and seek to build fellowship as much as Bible knowledge. Our groups range in intensity from "sanctified coffee breaks" to "cut-throat discipleship." An intensity match should be sought that contributes to harmony and challenge in the relationship.

A fourth and final factor is MATURITY. As mentioned earlier, an accountability partnership is not a relationship in which one disciples another. One is not the teacher and the other a student. A maturity match helps build a give-and-take relationship.

This does not mean one can not have more expertise in a certain area than the other. I have a graduate degree from a seminary and so know more details related to theology. My partner is a Certified Financial Planner whose knowledge of finances greatly eclipses mine. But when you look at each of

our overall lives, experiences, character, there is a maturity match. AVAILABILITY, AFFINITY, INTENSITY, MATURITY — is it required to have matches in all areas? How about "three out of four"? There are no "perfect matches," and slight differences should keep the relationship interesting and challenging. Substantial differences will probably make it frustrating!

❏ *People Who Make Good Partners*

Through my experience and listening to others, I've also identified some personal characteristics that should mark the lives of accountability partners. The first is confidentiality. As the relationship grows, there will be not only a discussion of goals and priorities, but strengths and weaknesses will be revealed — not exactly the items that should be aired to others. Each partner should honor the relationship by respecting the confidentiality of what is heard and the ability to assume it will go no further unless permission is sought first.

We all have within us that natural urge to "tell just one or two other people" what we've learned. It takes discipline to resist the temptation to share confidential matters with "just one other person." Most gossip spreads not by one person telling many others, but as a chain reaction. Someone tells one person, who tells just one other, who also tells another — and on it goes. Pick a partner who can honor the confidentiality of the relationship and you be a partner that does the same!

If you are married, be cautious not to violate the confidentiality of the marriage relationship when sharing with your accountability partner. This is not the place to dump your marital concerns and announce how good it would be if your spouse would just "shape up." The focus of accountability is your behavior, not your spouse's shortcomings!

A second helpful quality in partnerships is consistency. Nothing is more frustrating than cancelling appointment times or failure to follow through. While occasional lapses are perfectly understandable, this commitment must be a priority that doesn't take a back seat to all sorts of other pressing demands.

My partner and I are busy people with multiple responsibilities. Yet in the years we've been accountability partners, we've averaged moving or changing our appointments two or fewer times a year. That consistency signals to each of us that in the midst of other pressing demands, our partnership remains a priority.

Last but not least, the partnership should not only allow but encourage caring confrontation. Confronting one another in love is foundational to real effectiveness. Partners must be willing to risk "speaking the truth in love" (Ephesians 4:15) and the relationship should serve to "spur one another on toward love and good works" (Hebrews 10:24).

Telling the truth is harder than it sounds, or everyone would do it! It takes a secure self-esteem that is willing to risk rejection. It takes patience and tact so that the truth is given in a way that builds up, not tears down. Confrontation involves monitoring both my mouth and my spirit.

If confrontation is absent, a partnership will gradually become superficial. Honesty has a way of deepening all relationships and especially accountability relationships. "The kisses of an enemy may be profuse, but faithful are the wounds of a friend" (Proverbs 27:6).

 *The Accountability Meeting*

It is the people that make the accountability relationship effective. There is no program or process that will substitute for people of character. Once partners have been selected and a commitment to accountability has been made, a little structure is beneficial.

How the accountability meeting is structured is certainly open to variation but there should be a predetermined format. Without the discipline of an agenda, the session becomes more of a social hour than a time for accountability. It's amazing how "social" we can become and how easy it is to forget the purpose of the meeting, especially when we haven't been meeting our goals!

Let me share the typical format my partner and I use. We begin with one person reading down through his "Ten Most Wanted List", stopping after each goal to say whether it has been reached. If a goal has not been reached, an explanation is offered (notice I said explanation, not excuse!) and it is discussed. Then the other person covers his list completely. We take turns going first in reading our lists — one meeting I go first, Paul does so the next.

When we first started our partnership, we didn't share a lot beyond our goal lists. As our relationship has developed, we have followed the discussion of our "Ten Most Wanted List" by sharing more personally about our overall lives. We talk about what is going on in our private worlds — where we're experiencing stress, problems we're encountering, lessons we're

learning, and blessings we're receiving.

We conclude our time together by each praying for the other and both praying for the continued effectiveness of our accountability partnership. The meeting usually takes place in one of our offices so that we have the privacy we need for discussion and prayer. It takes no more than an hour, and afterwards we often go to lunch to share more casually together. We average meeting together for accountability once every two weeks.

The key elements of an accountability session are:

1. Review of goals
2. Sharing of overall well-being
3. Prayer

These elements keep the meeting on track. Without them, accountability times can degenerate into gossip sessions, pity parties, or opportunities to critique everyone and everything but each other. When these happen, the meeting becomes not only unproductive, but counterproductive to spiritual growth.

❏ *A Covenant Of Commitment*

Accountability partners should covenant to meet together for a specific period of time. In my partnership with Paul, we agree to meet together for a period of one year. At the end of each year, we conduct our annual accountability "audit", and then decide whether the relationship continues to provide accountability.

It's helpful to have a specific duration identified because each time it expires provides an opportunity to evaluate the partnership. It may be best to end the accountability relationship and seek a new partner. This does not mean, of course, that the relationship should cease — it is simply ending the accountability dimension. Having a specific time to end gives each person an "out" or an opportunity to renew the covenant for another year.

The covenant should also specify the frequency and regularity of the meeting times. We meet once every two weeks for about an hour each time. I know of partners who meet weekly and some who meet monthly. The "Iron Men" group of which I'm part meets every three weeks. A good starting point for most partnerships is a meeting once every two or three weeks.

The covenant of accountability is a serious commitment that should be honored. Many are tempted to step away from it, particularly when goals

are not being met. It's better to adjust the goals than stop the meetings. Because it is a substantial commitment, many will have a "trial period" of three months to test the compatibility of the partners and their ability to follow through. Christ spoke of "counting the costs" of discipleship before making a radical commitment, and forming an accountability partnership is certainly an excellent place to follow this command.

❏ *A Word Of Caution*

An accountability partnership can be a tremendous boost to personal and spiritual growth. A person who knows you and your goals well can greatly complement your discernment of the Lord's will for your life. He or she may well become a trusted confidant and advisor.

Let me wave a yellow flag! This person is not taking the Holy Spirit's place! Don't substitute his or her voice for God's voice speaking to your heart. A human's opinion is no match for God's conviction.

A little boy was scared to death by a thunderstorm. He quickly ran from his bed and crawled in with Mom and Dad. As Dad returned him to his own bed, he reminded his son that God was with him. The boy responded "I know God is with me, Dad, but right now I'd like something with skin on."

One of the values of accountability is that it provides someone with "skin on" to help us seek God's will and reinforce our will. Keep the focus on the lordship of Christ and remember that the partnership serves to prompt you in responding more completely to Him.

Now is the time to act. Can you list some potential partners? Once you've identified some possibilities, begin praying for God to guide you. Then take the risk of reaching out and initiating a partnership. Nothing ventured, nothing gained!

□ □ □ □ □ □ □ □

❏ *For Your Consideration:*

There is a difference between desire for relationships and commitment to relationships. All good relationships carry a price. Christ encourages us to "count the cost" of a relationship with Him. What are costs of a meaningful and lasting relationship?

An accountability partner is not . . .

An accountability partner is . . .

How would you describe a person to whom you "feel" accountable?

What are four factors this chapter mentions that should be considered when searching for an accountability partner or group?

What should be included in an accountability meeting? How would you structure a meeting to fit your needs and personality?

❏ ❏ ❏ ❏ ❏ ❏ ❏ ❏

Some accountability relationships don't work. How might a person end the "accountability" dimension while preserving the relationship?

❏ *Time to act:*

People I know who are potential accountability partners or could form an accountability group:

As I pray specifically about accountability, I will pray for:

I will approach somebody about an accountability relationship by _____(date).

12

Accountability Partnerships:

Questions and Answers

Yvonne Prowant

"Accountability partnerships are as unique as the individuals involved. There is one common thread — they have been vital in each partner's personal growth."

Perhaps you're wondering whether or not accountability partnerships really work. I'd like to share with you the most frequently asked questions and some testimonies from those who have accountability partnerships. Keep in mind that there are no "hard and fast" answers for every situation, for each partnership is unique. The following are offered as guidelines:

❑ *What information should and shouldn't be shared?*

Remember that the focus of this accountability partnership is individual accountability for each partner. If you have a goal which impacts others, the focus needs to be on your response or actions. Sharing about private matters, about a spouse for instance, should be limited. I try to use the rule of thumb that I'm willing to share anything that I know my husband would

131

be willing to tell my accountability partner himself.

I also think about what the impact of the information will be. Will she respect him less or have a negative opinion of him based on this information? I had a business acquaintance one time who shared some very personal information about her husband with me. None of it was positive. Some of it even involved areas of sin. Even though I never shared this with another person and tried not to be judgmental, I found it difficult to respect him. I noticed this most when he taught a Sunday School class that I attended. His teaching was inconsistent with what his wife had told me about his lifestyle.

What if I'm not making progress toward a goal?

Find out why and fix it. For the first or second meeting with your accountability partner, when you don't make progress toward a goal, look at your circumstances. Is there a time constraint, a temporary deadline that overrides other goals, illness, family crisis, or other events that are temporary barriers? If this is discovered, postpone your goal, then make a decision about when you will actively go back to your action plan.

If you cannot identify a temporary circumstance which is keeping you from progress, look at your action plan. Drop some of the actions that you think are not working and add other actions that would help you achieve your goal. This is why you should keep that list of possible actions when you develop your action plan.

If you have tried several different actions and can identify no particular barrier, then you need to ask yourself one of the hardest questions of all which requires complete honesty: How motivated am I to achieve this goal? And further ask yourself these questions: Do I really want this enough to do something about it? Why did I set this goal? Unless you come to the decision that you do want to achieve the goal and know why it's important to you, you probably won't make progress. Drop the goal at this point.

Your accountability partner plays a vital role in (a) helping you analyze why you might not be making progress and (b) offering suggestions for success. He or she may even ask you "Do you really want to do this?" or "Why have you established this as your goal?"

What if we're not able to meet?

Find a way. One of the best strategies to avoid repeated missed meetings is to decide on a regular meeting time at the beginning of your partnership. Then schedule this time together as you would any other

appointment. Of course, there may be times when emergencies come up or when schedule conflicts occur. Ideally, in such cases the meeting should be rescheduled for the earliest possible time. If that is not possible, perhaps a phone conference would suffice until your next face-to-face meeting. If repeated cancellations or missed appointments occur, it is time to evaluate the partnership and look for problems that should be addressed.

What if we never get around to talking about our accountability issues?

Make such talk a priority! At the beginning of your partnership, decide on a general format for your meetings. Then follow that format. If you find that you spend too much time up front socializing or catching up with each other, then plan your meetings to allow for that or meet separately for accountability and socializing. With one of my accountability partners we had a mutual goal of exercising. We met faithfully to exercise together with the idea that we were meeting for accountability and exercise. We exercised and between our steps and jumps, we would ask each other how things were going. By the wildest stretch of the imagination this really wasn't serving as a consistent accountability partnership for anything other than exercise. We recognized that and set aside a time separate from our exercise periods.

What if our accountability develops into a friendship?

An accountability partner who is also a friend is wonderful! — if you can both maintain an objectivity that is necessary for an effective accountability relationship. Remember that one of the reasons friends are so special to us is that they love us just the way we are. Friends who can do that and yet ask you questions and hold you accountable for the difficult areas of your life would be invaluable. If you evaluate your accountability partnership and discover that it is more of a friendship than an accountability partnership, then keep the friendship and find another accountability partner.

What if someone asks me for information about my accountability partner?

Don't tell them. Remember that one of the basic foundations of this partnership is confidentiality. It is vital. A general rule of thumb is that nothing should be shared that is not common, public knowledge. Many people feel uncomfortable when asked a personal question that they feel is

information that should not be shared and yet feel obligated to the person who asks the question. You have no obligation to the person asking the questions and he/she is the one who is out of line by asking. In my position as a manager, I handle a lot of confidential information, particularly as it relates to employee behavior or disciplinary process actions. When asked questions that would require me to violate confidences, I have a somewhat standard response: "I'm not allowed to share the information that you're requesting. If you have a need to know that, why don't you ask the person involved?" I don't know how many actually go to the person in question but I know that I usually get no further requests of this nature from the one asking. It keeps me accountable. Trying to remember who I told what in order to cover my bases is just not a game I want to play.

What if my accountability partner and I have a personality clash?

It might be a problem. This may be a touchy situation, but can be handled by an honest assessment of the partnership by each partner.
It will probably require some face-to-face discussion of the issues at hand. God made each of us unique. Focus on your feelings rather than accusing the other's behavior. You need to come to an agreement about whether the personality clash hinders your ability to meet the goals of your accountability partnership.

My spouse and I are very close. Why shouldn't we be accountability partners with each other?

Because it *seldom works.* Of course we are accountable to our husband or wife for certain areas of our lives, but the one-on-one accountability partnership, as designed, is not intended for spouses. Perhaps this is for some of the same reasons why your best friend may not be your wisest choice of an accountability partner. As we said in the chapter on goals, it is important for each spouse to know of the other's goal, but the process is not meant for spouses. First, I believe that men and women look at and react to situations differently. While it may be important to get a spouse's opinion or advice, the accountability partner will add additional insight into the problem solving process. Secondly, accountability partners should be at similar maturity levels. This may or may not be true for spouses. This may limit the freedom for dialogue about difficult issues. As a wife, I appreciate my husband's having someone with whom he can be

challenge him to grow in areas of his life that I would resort to nagging about if left to me.

How will I know when to end an accountability partnership?

You'll know it. There are definite symptoms of a partnership that is not effective. Some of these include frequently missed meetings, meeting but not discussing accountability issues, breach of confidentiality, meeting regularly yet not progressing toward your goals, or one sided growth. There is an evaluation form in the study guide that should be used to do regular assessments of your partnership. It should also be used any time you notice the above symptoms or just have the feeling the partnership is not going right. It's good to identify what's going wrong and make decisions about changes that are necessary.

How should I end an accountability relationship?

Speak the truth in love. It should start with an assessment of the partnership. It works best if each partner does one separately and then you come together to review it. If you have set a goal for the partnership at the beginning, it's helpful to go back to this goal and decide whether you're progressing toward that goal. It should end by mutual agreement. If there are questions in your mind, take a break. Decide not to meet for a period of time and see what happens. Commit the partnership to prayer during this time.

In one of my accountability partnerships, we were unable to meet because of circumstances for several weeks. When the circumstances reversed, we still did not meet. Finally we came together and decided that though we missed the friendship, the lack of meeting for accountability had not made a significant difference because when we were meeting, we had drifted to the point of spending our time on friendship, not accountability.

I'll also tell you how not to end accountability partnerships. Don't just let them die a slow death. If there are problems, address them. Don't just ignore the other person. Avoiding the issue will only prolong the pain. Don't use what I call the "hire a confronter technique." Sending the message by way of someone else is not fair. It takes a lot of courage to be honest, but it's worth the effort. Here's a quote from someone who recently ended an accountability relationship:

"In January, when it was time for our annual audit, we met first to

□ □ □ □ □ □ □ □

discuss what we wanted to be included in the audit. We came up with such things as:

- ❑ How do we feel about the past year?
- ❑ Did the relationship meet our expectations?
- ❑ Did we grow or reach some of our goals?
- ❑ Should this relationship end?

"We left that meeting with specific questions to both think about and pray about. It was a very helpful thing to do because the next two weeks we were focused on the same areas that would be discussed in our next meeting.

"Because of that, I feel strongly that the Lord was very much a part of our next time together. It was a time of open, honest sharing and because of specific areas of concern we chose to dissolve the relationship. The important thing we concluded was that even though the accountability relationship ended, the friendship was very important and that would not end. We even set times to get together. It was also important to us that we both seek new accountability relationships."

Does this really work??

Consider an example from the life of a school social worker:

"A look back to some of the very earliest goals makes me realize how we both have grown. Sometimes we don't see that growth at short glances but over a greater span of time it is very evident. For example, a concern in my life was my relationship with my adult step-children who have been unchurched. They do not live in my community. In fact, when we began to work on this accountability, two kids were living in Germany, one in Florida and two about an hour away. One was estranged due to matters in her own life. How could I in any real way impact them spiritually? The goals I set, with the help of my partner, were very practical. We determined that the Bible is unequivocal about the need for us, as Christians, to love God and love others. That love to others includes forgiveness, cheek turning, giving love even when it is not reciprocated. Scriptures and Bible stories must come to your mind quickly when I present those Biblical concepts.

"Because of those concepts, my goals were established regarding the

frequency I would pray for each of them. Also, I was held accountable for the frequency of my contact with them — whether via phone, letter, or visiting.

"I see changes in four of the five children which I feel relates directly to these activities. One met and married a gal in Germany who has been raised in the church . (She was even from his hometown!) One is dating a devout Christian who holds him at arms length, pending his own faith step. He travels across several states to maintain that relationship. One came with his family to live with us for several months -providing the opportunity to witness in lifestyle and words. They have returned to Germany, but our relationship is forever changed and in their time here, we all learned to love each other. The one, previously estranged, is now a Christian.

"God is still at work in their lives. I thank my friend and accountability partner for holding me accountable for my behavior towards them. With her, I can honestly admit my frustration and wish to give up at times. She understands even those lapses and challenges me in a new way each time we meet.

"I feel God honors the steps we take. These changes came about, not due to my effort, but due to God's grace and Spirit at work and simply through my willingness to be in harmony with His word."

❏ *Her Partner's Comments*

Lois' partner validates the value of this partnership. This quote also illustrates that while there are guidelines, each partnership needs to be designed to meet the needs of the individuals involved.

"Lois and I are an example of two women who work fulltime, lead busy lives in the church, with our families and school, and still manage to squeeze in an accountability relationship. The key to our relationship has been flexibility. At first we thought we had to meet once a week and adhere to a certain schedule — just like Pastor Wayne and Paul! That didn't work for us, but it did provide a framework.

"We have been together for three or four years now and have gone from meeting once a week to our current meetings of once a month. We started out with a 'Ten Most Wanted List' and also have used the Personal

Stewardship Inventory and the Personal Excellence Plan to get an idea of where we are and where we want to go. We spend our time together reviewing our goals, setting new ones for the next month (if needed), and then end our time in prayer. Sometimes our get-togethers are strictly business and sometimes they are combined with socializing.

"There have been many changes in each of us and in our relationship with one another. We have both gone through periods when we weren't sure we wanted to continue in the relationship and gave it a breather — but we were sure glad to get back together again! We didn't know how much it meant to us and how much we meant to each other until we took that time apart.

"Accountability has helped me to trust another person (something I struggle with) in their wisdom, confidentiality, and friendship. That has been my biggest area of growth. We are both able to freely express ourselves and to confront each other. Our accountability relationship has grown into a close friendship that will most likely last a lifetime."

❏ *Accountability Partners and Friends*

Following is an example of partners who have combined accountability and friendship:

"I had been thinking about having an accountability partner for sometime but couldn't decide who to ask. I really wished it could be a certain person, but she was so busy. I decided it would be an imposition to ask her. Then the phone rang. It was her asking me, of all things, to be her partner. I agreed if she would be mine, too.

"Usually we meet every other week for about two hours. One hour, more or less, is devoted to accountability. The other is devoted to sharing happenings, feelings and friendship.

"Every little while — it may be two weeks, one month, or six weeks — we revise the goals we have set. We may drop some, retain some, add some, or change some. In our accountability time we go over our goals, sharing what we are or aren't accomplishing and what we need to do about it. We are always excited when we have completed a goal and can replace

it with a new one.

"Our meetings are a time to which I look forward mostly with anticipation, but sometimes with embarrassment and concern.

"Accountability has caused me to be more conscious of setting and completing goals, more regular in my prayer life and Bible reading, and more committed in allowing Jesus to be Lord of my life.

"It has also helped me to make schedules and follow them in the routine and mundane things of life."

❏ *Prompted To Action*

Here's an example of a man who made a life changing decision and acted on it because of accountability.

"We meet every week for one hour. We have taken Wayne's suggestion of a word (or two) for the next year and keep each other accountable. That makes goal setting simpler and easier to follow up. My words for next year are simplicity and wisdom. My partner's are trust and patience!

"A story from a past accountability partner. I was thinking about going back to school to get my Masters. I was dragging my feet . . . for months and months. Finally he said, 'by next (two weeks) Thursday I want you to come to me with a decision . . . either this school or that and a course of study.' For two weeks, I researched, visited schools, made phone calls and finally decided to go to Western and get a Master's degree in clinical counseling. That Thursday I was very anxious to report to him 'my progress.'
"He stood me up and didn't make the appointment. Boy was I ripped but then God began to work on me. Who did I do all this for? Not for my partner but for me. The fact that he didn't show up made me realize that I made a decision to go back to school and his keepin' me accountable helped me make the decision. I'm still in my counseling classes today because of my accountability partner."

❑ *Good Intentions Become Daily Actions*

Following is a quote from a gentleman in our church who is recognized as spiritually mature. For him accountability made the difference in the important areas of his life that were not obvious to others.

"I've been a Christian for a lot of years. I was always lacking in consistent Bible reading and meaningful prayer. It's amazing how God has used my partner and my accountability relationship to vastly improve myself in these critical areas. His growth in these and other areas of life have been encouraging also.

"Facts: We've been friends for eight to ten years. We meet every other Monday at 4:00 p.m.

"Format: prayer; ask each other's goals one by one (yes or no); analyze results and look for ways to improve a 'struggling goal(s)'; closing prayer; fellowship.

"Accountability definition: 'Putting our good intentions into godly actions.'

"The accountability class I took was very helpful in knowing the proper way to have an organized and effective accountability relationship."

❑ *For Your Consideration:*

How did someone encourage you along the way toward the achievement of a goal?

❑ ❑ ❑ ❑ ❑ ❑ ❑ ❑

How have you offered encouragement to others?

For what areas of your life would you not want your spouse to hold you accountable?

What "safe" information would you start sharing when beginning an accountability partnership?

What action would you take if you sensed that the accountability partnership wasn't working?

What other questions do you have about how this accountability partnership works?

The Church And Accountability

Wayne Schmidt

"Accountability is crucial to the growth of any church and of the people who form that church. That means accountability first and foremost to the Head of the Church, Jesus Christ."

I do not have a "green thumb." My wife Jan does the gardening and prefers that I stay away from her plants. I'm not sure if the fence around our garden is to keep the rabbits out or keep me out — we both represent a threat to the garden's well-being!

But even with my limited knowledge of horticulture, I do know that atmospheric conditions must be right in order for a plant to flourish. The proper amount of moisture, heat and light can make the difference between a shriveled, unproductive plant and one that is thriving and fruitful.

This is also true of the local church. I believe that since its inception God has desired that the local church be a place for Christians to flourish and bear fruit. The fellowship of a local church ideally provides an atmosphere conducive to personal and spiritual growth.

As a pastor, I seek to constantly monitor the atmospheric conditions of the local church I serve. How easily it can become polluted with discouragement, bitterness, or preoccupation with power and position. I must ask "Does our church reinforce spiritual or sinful behavior? What are

we doing to help people take new steps forward in their walk with Christ? Is there a sense of anticipation that God will work in us and through us?"

Accountability is crucial to the growth of any church and of the people who form that church. That means accountability first and foremost to the Head of the Church, Jesus Christ. We submit to His authority and exist to please Him. It is also accountability to one another, for together we make up the body of Christ. We are dependent upon one another — all of us are necessary and should all be valued (1 Corinthians 12:12-27).

How does accountability take root in the life of a church?

Our church is still struggling to answer that question. We certainly have not "arrived," but are striving to strengthen its place in our fellowship and have identified some key elements along the way.

❑ *Nothing Rises Above The Level Of Leadership*

God's will for His Kingdom is accomplished often through human leadership. While we may struggle with God's design when frustrated by the failure of leaders, it is nonetheless His design. Nothing rises above the level of leadership, and that includes a commitment to accountability. If accountability is to be a integral part of a church's atmosphere, it must be practiced by a church's leader.

As a pastor, I believe that begins with me. When working with others in designing our congregation's philosophy of ministry, we made sure we included the priority of accountability. That means every time our philosophy of ministry is read or discussed, whether in board meetings, new member classes, planning sessions, leadership recruitment, or visitor orientation times, accountability is again and again brought to our attention.

I mention the subject of personal growth and accountability from the pulpit on a consistent basis. I pull illustrations from my personal accountability partnership and my small group experiences to constantly remind the congregation of my personal commitment. I talk about areas where I'm struggling and areas where I'm seeing progress that are being addressed through accountability. My preaching includes the challenge to accountability as well as the "how-to's" of building accountability into life.

We do attempt to build accountability into our church leadership structure. The Board of Elders is accountable to the members and the

members are accountable to their elected leaders. The Elders practice mutual accountability for their personal lives and church responsibilities. We attempt to implement accountability in our various lay ministry programs. Is it functioning perfectly? No. Before a recent accountability roundtable (I'll let you know what that is later in this chapter) I was reminded that there is yet ground to be gained. Here is a letter I received.

"I would like you to consider group to group, ministry to ministry, mutuality, staff to ministry, staff to congregational advisory groups as you consider accountability. I fear we are far too focused at KCC on individual fulfillment. I have thought at times in the accountability process that we may tend to become overachieving, compulsive, Christian yuppies. At what point do we stop and say 'enough about me?' Then, can we say 'What about God at work through me in ministry?' Who at the staff or board level knows ministries well enough (as well as accountability partners know each other) to supervise, encourage meaningfully and help in goal setting as well as limit setting? The question is not which one person knows ME, but who in ministry knows me IN MINISTRY?

"There can be a tremendous sense of isolation in lay ministry. If you have the skill and drive . . . DO IT! We'll let you FLY. You're on your own and in the end times Jesus will judge and give you feedback. I don't think that to be the total biblical message. Rather, 'Let us consider how we can spur one another on toward love and good deeds. Let us not give up meeting together as some are in the habit of doing. But let us encourage one another, and even more so as we see the day approaching.'

"Don't you find it interesting, Wayne, that you do have accountability in the accountability ministry as represented by this roundtable discussion which occurs several times a year? Is such a forum available for those in other areas of ministry? And what makes this one dynamic and effective? Just ideas to consider.

"What will be required to move KCC's mission of a church demonstrating Adoration, Acceptance and Accountability from an individual focus to a corporate focus so that such behaviors and attitudes represent the relationship between the board and ministries, the staff and lay ministry areas?

"To apply these concepts only to individual needs is to keep us all isolated, superficial and unconnected with the mission of the church. These are my first draft thoughts on the question but I present it as an arena for future focus and debate."

And yes, the letter was signed. Unsigned letters don't represent good accountability, so I usually ignore them! This letter motivated me to talk with our church staff about providing support and accountability as people serve the Lord through our church.

❏ *Avenues Of Accountability*

Not only must church leaders challenge and instruct, but there must also be opportunities to take action. We like to provide a variety of accountability possibilities at various levels of intensity. Not every person is ready for an accountability partnership, but each person should be accountable at some level and seek to increase his or her accountability.

In our church, people first participate in a worship service, and because we are a larger congregation, people often find it to be a convenient place to "hide." There is more anonymity than accountability. So we encourage their next step to be a visit to one of our CONNECTIONS, where attendance is recorded and fellowship is encouraged. Often there is a small group time as part of the class period for the purpose of prayer, topic discussion, and forming relationships. Social events and other activities foster relationships which provide accountability.

A next step may be a small group. Some of our small groups have a less intense level of accountability so people participate as regularly as they desire. Other groups track attendance, follow-up on absentees, and monitor the spiritual commitment of participants. Our Navigator's 2:7 groups require homework and memorization, while our pastoral care groups are much more relaxed. Our accountability groups and partnerships are the most intense. They almost always involve setting and sharing goals in all areas of life. Confidential prayer concerns are exchanged with both strengths and weaknesses being revealed.

We encourage the people of our congregation to choose a level of accountability that slightly stretches them, and over time to grow into new levels of accountability. While prompting them to take the initiative, our CONNECTIONS and small groups are constantly recruiting people to

become involved. Many people desire multiple levels of accountability simultaneously. That is true for me — I am part of the church board, a pastoral care group, a CONNECTION, a men's accountability group (IRON MEN) and a 1:1 partnership. Some of us just require more help than others!

❏ *Assisting Accountability Relationships*

Not all accountability relationships work. Sometimes they fail to flourish because there is not a good match among the people involved. Sometimes a person or the people involved have a change in circumstances that causes them to alter their commitment. Failure may result, however, even in potentially productive relationships without the proper support a local church can offer. We have identified three areas that contribute to frustration — a lack of knowledge, lack of experience and lack of support — the local church can address each of these needs.

❏ *What You Don't Know Can Hurt You*

Many times accountability relationships suffer because of a lack of knowledge of the "basics." People may have misinformed expectations of what the relationship should be, not know how to properly establish goals and priorities, or not understand the dynamic nature of the commitment.

Some of this knowledge comes by "trial and error." Every accountability relationship is different and so may operate under different "ground rules." But much that characterizes good accountability is common to all accountability experiences. When I first started encouraging our church toward accountability, I failed to provide the necessary "how-to's" that would have been helpful. That's when Yvonne talked with me about designing a class that would systematically communicate the principles and practices of accountability. It is out of that class curriculum that this book developed, which we trust will further equip the people of our congregation as well as those in other churches.

Some come to the accountability class having already chosen a partner. Others come to learn more about what to look for before making their selection of which format for accountability is best for them. This class has helped more relationships of accountability succeed because of the insight it provides.

❑ *We Need Someone With Experience*

Experience is one of life's best teachers. A mark of wisdom is that we learn not only from our own experiences, but from the experiences of others. If some accountability relationships struggle due to lack of knowledge, others travel over bumpy roads due to a lack of experience that provides understanding for problem-solving.

Like all relationships, accountability partnerships require adjustments and from time to time face problems. If these problems aren't addressed, they can fester and cause additional difficulties. At times the experience needed to diagnose and heal the dilemma has not yet been personally achieved.

We as a church are attempting to develop a group of "accountability advisors." These are people more experienced in accountability relationships who can offer objective insight into the problems those with lesser experience may be facing. Experienced partnerships can mentor new partnerships, serving as enablers in the initial stages of a new relationship's development. They can also assist in the dissolving of an accountability partnership that is unproductive. It's painful to phase out the accountability dimension of a relationship even though the friendship can and should continue. Advisors can help overcome the initial discomfort, help identify some potential reasons the accountability did not grow, and encourage those involved to try again with other partners. While dissolving a partnership is a last resort, it is sometimes necessary and advisors can be of assistance.

❑ *The Accountability Roundtable*

Sometimes accountability partnerships suffer due to lack of knowledge, other times due to lack of experiences, and often it is just a matter of needing support. Recognizing this need, we provide an Accountability Roundtable to help support those in accountability partnerships.

The Roundtable, as the name suggests, is a place of mutual learning, problem-solving and rejoicing. It meets about once a quarter and everyone practicing or considering accountability is encouraged to attend. Although somewhat unstructured, there is usually an informal and flexible agenda that is followed.

We begin with introductions and a one-minute overview of each

person's accountability situation. Often at this point one participant will take note of another participant with whom he or she can relate and seek that person out after the Roundtable meeting.

Then we usually tackle an "issue." My accountability partner and I usually moderate the discussion but everyone's participation is encouraged. We've discussed relevant issues such as:

❏ Brainstorming ways in which people can locate a suitable accountability partner.
❏ Ways to make accountability attractive to people who may be apprehensive about it. How to evaluate an accountability relationship and end it if necessary (while remaining friends).
❏ How to protect confidentiality and respond when it is breached.
❏ What personality styles have the greatest possibility for compatibility in a partnership.
❏ How to find the balance between friendship and accountability.
❏ How to respond when a person fails to reach his or her goals.
❏ How to provide accountability not only for actions, but thoughts.

It's valuable to gain a variety of perspectives on these and other issues that impact the effectiveness of accountability.

We usually conclude with the sharing of experiences — humorous moments, defeats, victories, progress made — whatever may encourage or enlighten others. Let me share a few with you:

"It was very challenging to me to admit part of my goals were not realistic for me. I don't like to admit I'm pushing/expecting too much of myself. I realized it a couple weeks earlier, but taking action to modify the goals was difficult for me. However, moving from 'no' to being able to accomplish the goal is better for me spiritually, emotionally, and physically. I don't feel beaten."

"Prior to my accountability relationship I had a devotional life built on lots of 'good intentions' and guilt for not following through with those good intentions. In the beginning of our relationship I would occasionally meet the goals I had set for myself, usually so that I could say 'yes' to the goal — a matter of pride. Presently I will want to meet the goals that I have set for myself to please the Lord. I realize that pleasing the Lord is trying to get the most out of my goals as possible. For example, one of the goals I have is to

read through the One Year Bible. It's so easy to daydream and still have read through the day's reading. Now I really try to see what God wants me to learn from what I am reading. That means more concentration while I study."

"On one occasion we met in a restaurant and decided to pray in one of our cars. It was a cool day and when we looked up from praying the windows were all steamed up. It was uncomfortable having two guys get out of a car with the windows steamed!"

"We are two different people and the Lord allows us to complement each other. She helps me be flexible, I help her be concrete."

"I've never been one to make goals (let alone obtain them), so accountability has really helped me in this area. I've had the chance to realistically look at each area in my life and see what's doing okay (affirming) and what needs some attention."

"My partner and I put our families at a higher priority than our meetings. Often Satan uses this to discourage us. We get lazy if we can't meet as often or as long as we wish. (It has helped us get right to the point and discuss our goals.) It also tends to mix our other "friendship times" with mini-checkups; example — an extra phone call or card to help encourage us with our goals."

"What I most enjoy is the regular, planned opportunity to fellowship with my accountability partner about those things most meaningful and important to me as a Christian. We discuss not only our goals, but also our discoveries in Bible study and/or prayer, and what God has been doing in our lives since we last met. Often, it is not until this "review" time that I realize that God was active in the middle of something that happened."

The sharing of experiences help us develop realistic expectations of our accountability relationships.

❏ *Beginning Is Half Done*

Several years ago I had the privilege of attending a conference at the Crystal Cathedral at which Dr. Robert Schuller spoke. While not seeing eye-

to-eye with him on everything, I've always found him to be an inspiration. He is known for his ability to create and communicate simple statements that have profound impact.

One of those statements is "Beginning is half done." It acknowledges that the toughest part of any new endeavor is its initiation. Once action is taken, momentum builds and good things result.

Why not start now! Begin your own relating of accountability! How about taking the initiative to become part of a group? Or maybe a one-to-one partnership would be better for you. Just do something! How about prayerfully setting some goals and letting another help you reach them? Does all this sound interesting to you? Want to start? Then let's go . . . Beginning is half done!

❏ *For Your Consideration:*

Every church has an "atmosphere" — often visitors can sense it the moment they walk through the doors. What kind of "atmosphere" stifles the growth of a church and its members? What kind of "atmosphere" stimulates the growth of a church and its members?

What does 1 Corinthians 12:12-27 have to say about our mutual dependence upon each other in the body of Christ?

What are ways a local church can encourage accountability among its members?

❏ ❏ ❏ ❏ ❏ ❏ ❏ ❏

In your local church, what activities carry:
Minimal accountability?

Medium accountability?

Maximum accountability?

Like all relationships, accountability partnerships require adjustments from time to time. What kinds of adjustments may be necessary?

❏ *Time to act:*

I can help my church encourage accountability by: (specific action)

"Beginning is half done." The starting point for me to apply what I've learned in this book is: